Community
and Social Change
in America

Community and Social Change in America

Thomas Bender

Clarke A. Sanford–Armand G. Erpf
Lecture Series on Local Government
and Community Life

Rutgers University Press
New Brunswick, New Jersey

Publication of this book was partially supported by a grant from the Arkville Erpf Fund and Roswell Sanford.

LIBRARY OF CONGRESS CATALOGING IN PUBLICATION DATA

Bender, Thomas.
  Community and social change in America.

  (Clarke A. Sanford–Armand G. Erpf lecture
series on local government and community life)
  Includes bibliographical references and index.
  1. United States—Social conditions.
2. Community. 3. Social change. I. Title.
II. Series.
HN57.B455   301.34′0973   78–1677
ISBN 0–8135–0858–4

To Sally

Contents

Foreword

The Clarke A. Sanford–Armand G. Erpf Lecture Series on Local Government and Community Life was initiated at the State University of New York Agricultural and Technical College at Delhi to stimulate research and scholarship. Each lecture is expanded into a book that is expected to enrich the literature of the social sciences.

The series was originally founded to perpetuate the memory of Clarke A. Sanford, who for more than sixty years was a rural New York newspaper editor and publisher, an active conservationist and naturalist, and a civic leader in the Catskill Mountain region of New York State. The Sanford lectures were made possible by his son and colleague, Roswell Sanford, and his longtime friend Armand G. Erpf, a senior partner in Loeb Rhodes, Inc., who was instrumental in creating the movement to preserve the history, culture, and environment of the Catskills. After Mr. Erpf's death in 1971, the lecture series was renamed the Clarke A. Sanford–Armand G. Erpf Lecture Series. Both men shared the belief that free and good government has to be rooted in strong local government and community life; the purpose of the series is to focus scholarship on local government and community life toward that end.

On October 12, 1976, Dr. Thomas Bender, Associate Professor of History at New York University, and a 1975 winner of the Frederick

Jackson Turner Prize from the Organization of American Historians, delivered the bicentennial Sanford–Erpf lecture at Delhi on the changing meaning of community in American history. That lecture has been expanded into this book. Dr. Bender's study is a significant bicentennial contribution to the social sciences. When delivered at the college, the lecture immediately drew a wide range of reactions and achieved what the Sanford–Erpf series seeks to encourage, that is, new insights and approaches that, when put forth in the market-place of ideas, stretch the parameters of human understanding and knowledge.

In the pages that follow, Bender sets out to "stimulate new under-standings of the place of community in the past and present." Well-established sociological concepts of community and society—Tön-nies' *Gemeinschaft* and *Gesellschaft*—are reexamined to provide the basis for reinterpretation of their popular historical applications. Bender uses a historical account of changing patterns of social rela-tions to assess the place of community in people's lives.

What does Bender say all this means? In brief, he contends it means the transformation of society, from a simple agrarian com-munity in early American history, to a more complex urban and market-oriented life in which the experience of community is still both possible and necessary. For those who lament the passing of small-town America and the virtues associated with rural life, Ben-der shapes a raison d'être and conceptual framework in which to place the past and with which to experience the present and future. Many social scientists will find this thesis offers a provocative, new social history that could recast present understandings of many con-temporary problems.

Seldon M. Kruger
Vice President for Academic Affairs
State University of New York
Agricultural and Technical College
Delhi, New York

Preface

This book is a historical and theoretical exploration of the changing structure and meaning of community in American history. I hope through it to accomplish three things: to consider how social theory relates to the experience of community in American history, to offer a narrative structure for historical considerations of community in the American past, and to contribute to the contemporary discussion of the problem and prospects of community in modern America by offering a historical perspective on it.

Constraints inherent in the length and format of this book (matters largely dictated by the book's origin) carry a certain risk: The argument is long enough to whet the reader's appetite for the details and qualifications that space does not allow, but given my purpose, which is to be suggestive rather than definitive, the risk seems worth taking. I propose to provoke new questions, perspectives, and understandings on community in American history and, far from settling questions, to open up the topic to more fruitful historical research.

I have many debts that I wish to acknowledge here. An invitation to be the Sanford–Erpf Lecturer for 1976 at the State University of New York Agricultural and Technical College at Delhi began this book. I want to express my thanks for that invitation and for the opportunity to present my ideas in a public lecture as well as to discuss them with students and faculty there. This book would never have come into being were it not for an act of unusual thoughtfulness and generosity on the part of my colleague, Patricia Bonomi, and I am deeply appreciative. Three graduate students at New York University helped me in various ways as I brought the book toward completion, and I want to thank Gary Chapman, Timothy Coogan, and, especially, Jeffrey Eichler, who, not only helped me with some crucial research, but who was always a challenging critic in our discussions of the project. Finally I want to thank several friends and colleagues who read earlier versions of the manuscript: Lawrence Chenoweth, Michael Frisch, Paul Mattingly, Richard Sennett, and Wilson Smith. Through stubbornness or incapacity, I have failed to follow all of their suggestions or heed all their warnings (and they should therefore be absolved from any responsibility for what follows), but I benefited a great deal from them.

Summer 1977
New York City

Abbreviations

The following abbreviations are used to signify journals frequently cited in the notes.

AA	*American Anthropologist*
AHR	*American Historical Review*
AJS	*American Journal of Sociology*
APSR	*American Political Science Review*
AQ	*American Quarterly*
ASR	*American Sociological Review*
CSSH	*Comparative Studies in Society and History*
HEQ	*History of Education Quarterly*
HER	*Harvard Educational Review*
HMN	*Historical Methods Newsletter*
HT	*History and Theory*
JAH	*Journal of American History*
JIH	*Journal of Interdisciplinary History*
JSH	*Journal of Social History*
JUH	*Journal of Urban History*
PP	*Past and Present*
RS	*Rural Sociology*
WMQ	*William and Mary Quarterly*

Community
and Social Change
in America

Chapter One

Introduction: The Meanings of Community

The notion of community has been central to the analysis of social and political life at least since Plato and Aristotle inquired into the character of the Greek polis, but the concept as found in modern scholarship is of more recent origin. The problem of community was one of the central concerns of the nineteenth-century social thinkers who were among the founders of sociology in Europe and the United States. Modernity, urbanization, and capitalism all seemed to threaten traditional patterns of social life. As they observed these processes, social analysts and philosophers began to discuss the problem of community in a way that raised a historical issue. How complete was the break with the past? What was the nature of that break? What form, if any, might community take under these radically new social circumstances? This concern, needless to say, has continued unabated into our own time, inside and outside of academic circles.

In both popular and academic discourse, the word *community* has quite positive connotations that are associated with visions of the good life. Yet there is, and always has been, an undercurrent of fear associated with the idea of community. Modern Americans fear that urbanization and modernization have destroyed the community that earlier shaped the lives of men and women, particularly in the small towns of the American past. Many popular discussions of alienation, anomie, and other supposed evils of modern urban life are extensions of this general worry about community. These popular concerns have been abetted, if not actually stimulated, by the writings of historians and sociologists that are laced with references to the "erosion," or the "decline," or the "breakup," or the "eclipse" of community under the impact of urbanization and modernization.

Has modern life in fact brought such a collapse? Can a historical perspective help us better to define our present situation? The historian can say definitely that if community is defined as a colonial New England town—and it frequently is defined that way—then the prospect of community today is indeed dim. Yet the historian should also note that to define community in such static terms is to ignore the process of history. Such a definition, moreover, tends to confuse a particular manifestation of community with its essence; its effect is to preclude the possibility of finding community in other times and places. Historical inquiry may enable us to clarify the precise character of the contemporary problem of community. In working toward this insight, the first task is the formulation of a definition of community that can accommodate historical change.

Most thinking about community, whether in academic social science or in popular attitudes, embodies a curious paradox. Statements about community assume a very definite past, but they are seldom genuinely historical in character. There is in such observations hardly any sense of the changing configurations of community over the course of American or European history. Very little attention is devoted to a consideration of the details of the actual processes of change in the structure and meaning of community over time. Instead a rather simple and direct relationship between past and present is assumed: In the past, there was community; in the present it has been (or is being) lost. Social change, for modern Americans, has come to mean the destruction of community. Perhaps one might find this process regrettable, but it is assumed nonetheless to be inevitable.

Within this rather closed logic of social explanation, there is really very little space for historical inquiry. By supplying an a priori answer to the problem of social change and community, this logic effectively defeats historical curiosity. Unfortunately, or fortunately, the processes of history are more complicated than these assumptions allow. Indeed, the more one tries to describe community in the present or in the past, the more important a historical consideration of the problem seems. When social analysts ignore the historical dimension, the result is a simplification and schematization of social change that weakens the explanatory power of even the most sophisticated theory. Any understanding of the fate of community in America today or at any time in the past depends upon an expansion of social theory to incorporate the concrete data of historical change into social explanation. For this to happen, however, we need a more complex and historically grounded account than we presently have of the American experience of community over a long period of time.

———————◆———————

The concept of community is, according to a recent historian of sociological theory, "the most fundamental and far-reaching of sociology's unit-ideas,"[1] yet it is also one of the most difficult to define. When a scholar undertook in 1955 to inspect and compare the definitions of community used in the literature of the social sciences, he found no fewer than ninety-four meanings given to the term.[2]

The most common sociological definitions used today tend to focus on a community as an aggregate of people who share a common interest in a particular locality. Territorially based social organizations and social activity thus define a community. A community is assumed to be a localized or microcosmic example of the larger

1. Robert Nisbet, *The Sociological Tradition* (New York: Basic, 1966), p. 47.
2. George A. Hillery, Jr., "Definitions of Community: Areas of Agreement," *RS*, 20 (1955): 118.

society.[3] The literature is not precise about the size of this territory. Apparently, it can range from a neighborhood, to a town, to a medium-sized city. In fact, there is no logical bar to making reference to New York City as a community. Although this definition has produced some very useful research, particularly in respect to locality-based social welfare organizations, the notion of New York City, or any other whole city in modern America, constituting a single community makes one pause.

Americans seem to have something else in mind when they wistfully recall or assume a past made up of small-town communities. This social memory has a geographic referent, the town, but it is clear from the many layers of emotional meaning attached to the word *community* that the concept means more than a place or local activity. There is an expectation of a special quality of human relationship in a community, and it is this experiential dimension that is crucial to its definition. Community, then, can be defined better as an experience than as a place. As simply as possible, community is where community happens.

Of course, a locality can be this kind of community. In colonial America, the town was a container of such communal relations, but there are other contexts for community besides the town and other territorial units. Territorially based interaction represents only one pattern of community, a pattern that becomes less and less evident over the course of American history. A preoccupation with territory thus ultimately confuses our understanding of community.

Even though community has been torn from its territorial mooring over the past three centuries of American history, the experience of community did not come to an end with this transformation in American social organization. To make this argument is not to deny the possibility of fundamental changes in the meaning and signifi-

3. For the best examples of this dominant approach to community studies, see Roland Warren, *The Community in America* (Chicago: Rand McNally, 1963); Albert J. Reiss, "Some Sociological Issues about American Communities," in *American Sociology*, ed. Talcott Parsons (New York: Basic, 1968), pp. 66–74; Talcott Parsons, *Structure and Process in Modern Societies* (New York: Free Press, 1960), pp. 250–279; and Conrad Arensberg and Solon Kimball, *Culture and Community* (New York: Harcourt, 1965).

cance of community for Americans; rather it is a way of documenting these changes by working toward a historically relevant and
usable definition of community.

Community, which has taken many structural forms in the past, is
best defined as a network of social relations marked by mutuality
and emotional bonds.[4] This network, or what Kai T. Erikson refers
to as the "human surround," is the essence of community, and it may
or may not be coterminous with a specific, contiguous territory.[5]
The New England town was a community, but it was not a definition of community. Similarly, a family, a neighborhood, a group of
friends, or a class can be a community without providing a definition of the concept. One must keep an open stance toward the
various structural forms that might contain community. A definition
of community must, therefore, be independent of particular structures.

A community involves a limited number of people in a somewhat
restricted social space or network held together by shared understandings and a sense of obligation. Relationships are close, often
intimate, and usually face to face. Individuals are bound together
by affective or emotional ties rather than by a perception of individual self-interest. There is a "we-ness" in a community; one is a

4. In the following preliminary definition, only direct quotations have specific cita-
tions. The position outlined in the next few paragraphs owes most to the following
works: Ferdinand Tönnies, *Community and Society,* trans. Charles P. Loomis (New
York: Harper, 1963); Max Weber, *The Theory of Social and Economic Organization,*
trans. Talcott Parsons (New York: Free Press, 1964); Robert M. MacIver, *Com-
munity: A Sociological Study* (New York: Macmillan, 1936); Robert Redfield, *The
Little Community* (Chicago: University of Chicago, 1955); Talcott Parsons, *The
Social System* (New York: Free Press, 1951); idem, *Structure and Process in Modern
Societies;* Roland Warren, ed., *Perspectives on the American Community* (Chicago:
Rand McNally, 1966); Rene König, *The Community* (London: Routledge & Kegan
Paul, 1968); Charles Tilly, *An Urban World* (Boston: Little, Brown, 1974); Robert
Nisbet, *The Quest for Community* (New York: Oxford University Press, 1969); idem,
The Social Bond (New York: Random House, 1970); idem, *The Sociological Tra-
dition;* Wilson Carey McWilliams, *The Idea of Fraternity in America* (Berkeley and
Los Angeles: University of California, 1973); and Martin Buber, *Paths in Utopia*
(London: Routledge & Kegan Paul, 1949).

5. See Kai T. Erikson, *Everything in Its Path: Destruction of Community in the
Buffalo Creek Flood* (New York: Simon & Schuster, 1976), esp. Introduction and
pt. III.

member. Sense of self and of community may be difficult to distinguish. In its deepest sense, a community is a communion. Martin Buber captured this quality when he wrote: "A real community need not consist of people who are perpetually together; but it must consist of people who, precisely because they are comrades, have mutual access to one another and are ready for one another."[6]

Men and women in a community share a fairly wide spectrum of their lives, though not necessarily everything. A community is people who, in the words of Robert MacIver, "share, not this or that particular interest, but a whole set of interests wide enough and complete enough to include their lives."[7] Hence communal relationships are diffuse in their concerns. They are not segmental relationships, and they are not oriented to narrow or specific ends. While a community is part of broader social aggregates, it remains a distinct social grouping. Far from being a microcosm of the whole society, it has a special quality that may result in tension with larger social aggregates. One's network of community, although it may not supply all the warmth and emotional support one needs, is an elemental fact of one's emotional life.

The solidarity that characterizes communities does not mean, however, that all is unity and harmony within. Many commentators err, I think, by insisting that absence of conflict be a part of the definition of community. Communal conflict, like the family conflict we all know, is real, though it differs from, say, market competition, in being mediated by emotional bonds.[8]

A community is an end in itself: It may offer aid or advantage to its members, but its value is basically intrinsic to its own existence. It does not exist to serve external or instrumental purposes. This

6. Buber, *Paths in Utopia*, p. 145.

7. Robert M. MacIver, *Society: Its Structure and Changes* (London: Long and Smith, 1932), pp. 9–10.

8. Weber saw community as the "antithesis of conflict" (Weber, *Theory of Social and Economic Organization*, p. 137). Charles H. Cooley, however, admitted that conflict existed in what he called "primary groups" and that the competition, passions, and conflicts that emerged in these groups were "socialized by sympathy" (Charles H. Cooley, *Social Organization: A Study of the Larger Mind* [New York: Scribner's, 1909], p. 23).

characteristic of community is related to a particular kind of social behavior identified by Max Weber as distinctively communal. He labeled a social relationship "communal" if its "orientation of social action . . . is based on a subjective feeling of the parties, whether affectual or traditional, that they belong together." He contrasted this with "associative" relationships, characteristic of modern political and economic institutions, that are based upon rational calculation of self-interest.[9]

No contemporary sociologist has written more frequently or more perceptively on community than Robert Nisbet. Perhaps it is therefore appropriate to conclude this preliminary definition with a quotation from him.

> Community is founded on man conceived in his wholeness rather than in one or another of the roles, taken separately, that he may hold in a social order. It draws its psychological strength from levels of motivation deeper than those of mere volition or interest. . . . Community is a fusion of feeling and thought, of tradition and commitment, of membership and volition. . . . Its archetype, both historically and symbolically, is the family, and in almost every type of genuine community the nomenclature of family is prominent.[10]

This definition, which harks back to the work of the classic nineteenth-century sociologists of community, captures an important dimension of popular attitudes, but it does not, as I have already noted, often turn up in the research reported today under the rubric of community sociology. Such bonds do not ordinarily characterize local social organization, so many sociologists, encouraged by aspects of modern social theory discussed in the next chapter, have assumed that modernization and urbanization have rendered this sort of community a thing of the past. This assumption has allowed research on locality-based action to be called "community sociology." Inasmuch as the local social relationships uncovered by this research are not community in the traditional sense, sociologists have developed a new term for these friendly but essentially casual

9. Weber, *Theory of Social and Economic Organization,* p. 136.
10. Nisbet, *Sociological Tradition,* pp. 47–48.

relationships: *community of limited liability*. Of course, there is nothing inappropriate about the development of this academic specialty that studies local life, but there is a curious, perhaps even pernicious, side effect. The identification of community with locality and communal experiences with rather casual associations has quietly redefined community in a way that puts it at odds with its historical and popular meaning.[11] This academic definition drains the concept of the very qualities that give the notion of community cultural, as opposed to merely organizational, significance.

The approach to community most often found in community sociology tends to divert attention away from the bonds of mutuality and sentiment that historically define the experience of community. Attention is instead focused on localities. This orientation is in part the product of a historical association dating from the 1920s linking community studies and rural sociology. Within the context of this sociological tradition, rural towns and farm neighborhoods were studied as communities. The assumed connection of rural towns with community was often supported by social experience, and it was universally compatible with the small town mythology that has been so influential in American history. But the assimilation of rural sociology into community sociology misdirected scholarship to a consideration of territory, rather than to the experience of community, as the object of sociological inquiry.

Because, as Kenneth Burke has observed, "A way of seeing is always a way of not seeing," this territorial image of community has consequences. It makes it difficult to see the networks of experience that in fact define community. If, by contrast, one assumes a different angle of vision that takes communal networks where one finds them, whatever their territorial arrangement, the chances of understanding the place of community in modern society and in American history are much enhanced. My intention is to suggest such new ways of seeing community.

11. On the notion of a locality-based community of limited liability, see Morris Janowitz, *The Community Press in an Urban Setting*, 2d ed. (Chicago: University of Chicago, 1967). For a slightly broader usage, derived in part from the work of Janowitz, see Scott Greer, *The Urbane View* (New York: Oxford University Press, 1972).

Once the notion of community is understood as a social network characterized by a distinctive kind of human interaction, it becomes possible to take community seriously as a historical phenomenon. One can talk about change without being trapped by the logic of collapse, and a number of interesting historical and sociological questions then open up. What structural forms have contained the experience of community in American history? How long and in what sense was the town a community? What form or forms does community take when the town no longer provides the primary context for community? What is the relationship of community to political and economic institutions? How do those relationships change with large-scale transformations in the structure of society?

———◆———

My method of pursuing these and similar questions has been consciously interdisciplinary. Historical scholarship is used as a fulcrum for critical analysis of social theory, while my historical narrative is explicitly attentive to theory. If, as I have indicated, much thinking about community is shaped by a paradigm of social change that is fundamentally ahistorical, I have tried to link theory and history more effectively. In line with Michael Katz's recent call to social historians, I am seeking to "formulate questions that will guide research in ways not only theoretically fruitful but historically appropriate."[12] The major theoretical fruit of this effort, if I have succeeded, is a historically grounded concept of community, while its historical contribution is an image of the past that enables us to see new dimensions of community and patterns of change in the experience of community.

The argument on the following pages is speculative and tentative. The evidence offered is illustrative and suggestive rather than definitive. It is an essay in hypothetical history, after the fashion of Bernard Bailyn's *Education in the Forming of American Society*.[13] My goal has been to use what we know about community in order to

12. Michael B. Katz, *The People of Hamilton, Canada West* (Cambridge: Harvard University, 1975), p. 9.

13. Bernard Bailyn, *Education in the Forming of American Society* (New York: Random House, Vintage, 1960).

develop new perspectives that will expand our knowledge of community in ways that can stimulate new understandings of the place of community in the past and present.

One observation concerning the historical generalizations I have made about Americans seems appropriate here. My references are to the vast majority of Americans who lived in towns, rather than to the small minority who lived in large cities. As late as 1870, the point where I begin referring to metropolitan experiences, there were only twenty-five places with a population of fifty thousand or more. Fewer than one-in-four Americans lived in places of twenty-five hundred or more. I hope, moreover, that my acknowledgments of possible alternative patterns of life deriving from class position or cultural heritage will protect me from the charge of homogenizing the past, for I have tried, admittedly, to describe modal patterns. Given the constraints of space, and the scholarship available, it is impossible to handle this problem otherwise. Readers, I expect, will easily see how my argument would apply to aspects of our past not specifically considered here.

This study emphasizes the changes in the structure of social relations much more than the changes in meaning that people gave to these structures. Wherever possible, I have suggested, even if in rather broad terms, these shifts in consciousness. The interaction of belief and social structure is very complex, however; it can be understood, if at all, only through detailed studies impossible in a brief book attempting to fill a broad canvas. In a subsequent study I plan to undertake such a cultural history. I note this problem here so that the reader will not infer from the emphasis in what follows that structural matters constitute the whole, or even the most important part, of the study of community in the past.

———◆———

Briefly, I develop my argument as follows. In Chapter 2, I consider aspects of the development of American social theory in the twentieth century, an appropriate starting point because this theory has largely shaped our sense of the relationship of community to the processes of social change in the past. After laying out the basic logic of this theory, I argue that its most common formulations, the ones best known to historians, have serious limitations as a guide to the understanding of community in American history or, for that matter, in the present. In contrast, by returning to the nineteenth-century origins of this theory, particularly to Ferdinand Tönnies's *Gemeinschaft–Gesellschaft* typology, one finds a surprising complexity and sensitivity to actual historical processes that is absent in many modern theories that derive from the work of Tönnies. It is possible, I propose, to recover these qualities and give them their due in modern social theory in a way that opens up fruitful lines of historical and sociological investigation.

With this theoretical work accomplished, I turn in Chapter 3 to the historiography and history of community in America. Much of the current historiography has weaknesses similar to those found in modern social theory, but reformulation is possible, and it becomes the task of this chapter. The theoretical orientation developed in Chapter 2 provides a perspective from which to sketch a history of the changing structure and meaning of community over a long period of time, from 1600 to 1900, in a way that opens up new and interesting historical questions about community while providing historical detail that adds richness to the theory. Chapter 4 builds upon this overview, or macroanalysis, of the changing place of community in American society, but the focus shifts to the individual and the family unit in my attempt to locate the various contexts of community available to the people within the social networks that provide the social texture of their lives. The epilog offers some observations on how the history and theories of community offered here relate to the search for community in contemporary America.

Chapter Two

Social Theory and the Problem of Community

Whether used as an analytical device for classifying social aggregates or as a normative judgment on social life, the concept of community never stands alone.[1] Rather, it is consistently used as one pole of a typology of social forms that implicitly or explicitly contrasts communal with noncommunal patterns of life, or more generally, premodern with modern society. This contrasting technique of defining modern society in relation to what went before dates back at least to the Renaissance,[2] but during the nineteenth century, coincident with the emergence of sociology, the technique was turned explicitly to the problem of explaining the social changes associated with urbanization and industrialization.

Within this intellectual tradition, urbanization is treated, virtually by definition, as disruptive of communal patterns of social life.[3] History from this perspective unfolds an inevitable social thesis: Social unity is shattered and communal solidarities are re-

1. This problem of usage is considered by Colin Bell and Howard Newby, *Community Studies* (New York: Praeger, 1972), chaps. 1–2.
2. See Frederick J. Teggart, *Theory of History* (New Haven: Yale University, 1925), chap. 8.
3. The definition of urbanization used here is a general one; many would equate it with modernization, as I essentially do in the following discussion. Charles Tilly expresses what I have in mind when he writes: "Urbanization implies changes . . . that follow from the increased involvement of the members of rural communities in sets of activities, norms, and social relationships that reach beyond the limits of their own localities" (Tilly, *The Vendée* [Cambridge: Harvard University, 1976], pp. 11–12).

placed with associations based upon interest. Conventional theory
and, for that matter, much Marxist analysis find their underlying
structure in this logic. The result is often an approach to social
change that is fundamentally ahistorical. Although sociology has
from its inception taken on the task of explaining a historical problem—the emergence of modern urban and industrial society—its
sense of the past is made up of ideal types linked only by logical
necessity. This logic conveniently supplies a history without obligat-
ing the theorist to analyze structural change as a temporally and
culturally situated process.[4] The manner in which this logic eludes
engagement with history warrants detailed consideration.

Typological Theories of Social Change

It is difficult to establish the precise beginnings of this tradition of
sociological thought. Most histories of social theory, however,
credit Sir Henry Maine with first formulating contrasting ideal
types as a device for studying social change. Maine undoubtedly
deserves the credit he has been given; his distinction between societies based upon "status" and those based upon "contract" was sys-
tematically worked out and imaginatively applied to the historical
record. Yet when Maine wrote in his classic *Ancient Law* (1861)
that "the movement of the progressive societies has hitherto been a
movement *from Status to Contract*,"[5] his concern was less with the
new pattern of *social* relationships that had emerged in the nineteenth century than with questions of law and political economy.
His argument that modernity brought a shift in the bases of social
organization from kinship, status, and joint property rights to territory, contract, and individual rights was a way of reading history so
that the legal and economic ideas of liberal capitalism identified
with Victorian England could be linked to and justified by the idea
of progress.[6]

4. Philip Abrams, "The Sense of the Past and the Origins of Sociology," *PP*, no. 55
(1972), p. 20.
5. Henry Maine, *Ancient Law*, 10th ed., cheap ed. (London: Murray, 1905), p. 151.
6. This was obvious to the Progressive intellectual Mary Parker Follett who, at
the beginning of the twentieth century, in arguing for a more collectivist political

Maine's *Ancient Law* and its sequel, *Village Communities in the East and West* (1871), found wide readership, and his concept of societal evolution was enormously influential. Eventually it was taken up by Ferdinand Tönnies, a young German scholar who was seeking to develop sociological concepts that would explain the changes in social relations that were associated with capitalism and the urbanization of society. Tönnies recognized in this typology analytic possibilities that offered a way of giving sociological form to Karl Marx's depiction of social change in the urban-industrial era as a process whereby "natural relationships" were dissolved "into money relationships."[7] In 1887, at the age of thirty-two, Tönnies offered his own ideal types when he published *Gemeinschaft und Gesellschaft*. With this publication, Tönnies introduced into the sociological literature a typology that has proven to be one of the discipline's most enduring and fruitful concepts for studying social change.

There are no exact English equivalents for *Gemeinschaft* or *Gesellschaft*, but they can be translated roughly as "community" and "society." Tönnies's definition of *Gemeinschaft* corresponds to the historical and popular notion of community; he offered family, kinship groups, friendship networks, and neighborhoods as examples of *Gemeinschaft* patterns of group solidarity. *Gemeinschaft*, he wrote, is characterized by "intimate, private, and exclusive living together." *Gesellschaft*, which he identified with the city, is an "artificial construction of an aggregate of human beings," characterized by competition and impersonality. Summing up the difference between these two forms of social relationships, he observed that in *Gemeinschaft*, people "remain essentially united in spite of all separating factors, whereas in *Gesellschaft* they are essentially

economy, contended that society had already gone from "status to contract" and was beginning to move from "contract to community." See Follett, *The New State* (New York: Longman's, 1920), p. 125.

7. Karl Marx, *The German Ideology*, ed. R. Pascal (New York: International Publishers, 1947), p. 57. For the influence of Maine, see Louis Wirth, "The Sociology of Ferdinand Tönnies," *AJS*, 32 (1926): 416.

separated in spite of all uniting factors."[8] Capitalist industrial production and the urbanization of society, he thought, involved an
evolution from a predominantly *Gemeinschaft* pattern of social relations to one dominated by *Gesellschaft*.

Since Tönnies and Maine wrote, similar dichotomies, with different terminology, have been common in sociological thinking concerned with the urbanization and modernization of societies. Emile
Durkheim referred to the shift from "mechanical solidarity" based
upon psychological consensus to "organic solidarity" founded upon
the interdependence resulting from the division of labor in modern
urban society. Among Americans, Charles Horton Cooley observed
early in the twentieth century that urban society is characterized by
impersonal "secondary" relationships that are analytically distinct
from the "primary," or face-to-face, relationships of the small village
or the family. More recently, Robert Redfield developed a typological distinction between "folk" and "urban" cultures.[9]

These dichotomies in their various forms, often subsumed under
the general rubric of the community-society continuum, became
central to the study of community in urbanizing societies.[10] The
turn-of-the-century founders of the academic discipline of sociology
in the United States were particularly interested in understanding
how the nation's burgeoning cities differed as social settings from
the small towns of American tradition and, in most cases, of their
own childhoods.[11] Their "programmatic question," as a recent critic
has put it, echoed that of their European predecessors: "How can
the moral order of society be maintained and the integration of its

8. Ferdinand Tönnies, *Community and Society,* trans. Charles P. Loomis (New
York: Harper, 1963), pp. 33, 64, 65.

9. Emile Durkheim, *The Division of Labor in Society,* trans. George Simpson
(New York: Free Press, 1933); Charles H. Cooley, *Social Organization: A Study of
the Larger Mind* (New York: Scribner's, 1909), chap. 3; and Robert Redfield, *The
Folk Culture of Yucatan* (Chicago: University of Chicago, 1941).

10. They are all discussed under this rubric in the *International Encyclopedia of
the Social Sciences,* ed. David L. Sills, 17 vols. (New York: Macmillan, 1968).

11. On the small-town origins of early American sociologists, see Roscoe Hinkle
and Gisela Hinkle, *The Development of Modern Sociology* (New York: Random
House, 1954), pp. 3, 17n.

members achieved within a highly differentiated and technological social structure?" It was "the problem of community in the New Age."[12]

As they probed the consequences of urbanization for community life as small-town Americans had known it, these scholars found Tönnies's conceptual framework useful. Identifying gemeinschaft with a somewhat idealized image of the small town, as Tönnies himself often did, American sociologists recognized what Tönnies defined as gesellschaft in New York, Chicago, and many lesser cities. The typological approach seemed to offer insight into the social transformation they were living through.[13] Robert Park, one of the early members of the sociology department at the University of Chicago and a founder of urban sociology, observed, for example, that the diverse terminology used to express the community–society continuum revealed that the concept was as yet unrefined, but he insisted that "the differences are not important. What is important is that these different men looking at the phenomenon from quite different points of view have all fallen upon the same distinction. That indicates at least that the distinction is a fundamental one."[14]

This tradition of urban theory culminates, in conventional accounts,[15] in the comprehensive statement on urban and community life contained in Louis Wirth's classic essay, "Urbanism as a Way of Life" (1938).[16] The typological approach developed by Tönnies

---

12. Claude S. Fischer, "The Study of Urban Community and Personality," *Annual Review of Sociology,* 1975, pp. 67–68.

13. On the place of gemeinschaft–gesellschaft theory in twentieth-century sociology, see Edward Shils, "The Contemplation of Society in America," in *Paths of American Thought,* ed. Morton White and Arthur Schlesinger, Jr. (Boston: Houghton Mifflin, 1970), pp. 397–400; and Werner J. Cahnman, "Toennies in America," *HT,* 16 (1977), 147–167. For a brief discussion of its use at Chicago, see Robert E. L. Faris, *Chicago Sociology, 1920–1932* (San Francisco: Chandler, 1967), pp. 43–48.

14. Quoted in Carle C. Zimmerman, *The Changing Community* (New York: Harper, 1938), p. 81.

15. For such an account, see Brian J. L. Berry, *The Human Consequences of Urbanization* (New York: St. Martin's, 1973).

16. Louis Wirth, "Urbanism as a Way of Life," *AJS,* 44 (1938): 1–24; reprinted in Albert Reiss, Jr., ed., *Louis Wirth on Cities and Social Life* (Chicago: University of Chicago, 1964), pp. 60–83.

provides the organizing framework for the essay.[17] At the outset, Wirth announced his perspective: He was going to view "urban-industrial and rural-folk society as ideal types of communities."[18] He then proceeded in the body of the essay to portray urbanization as a powerful social force modifying social relations in ways compatible with Tönnies's theory. Under the impact of the demographic variables he identified with urbanization (population, density, and heterogeneity), Wirth argued that communal ways broke down and were replaced by a new pattern of life that Tönnies had called *Gesellschaft* and that Wirth labeled "urbanism."

Under urban conditions, Wirth explained, social relations are "impersonal, superficial, transitory, and segmental." Functional roles are highly specialized and interdependent. "The distinctive features of the urban mode of life," Wirth insisted, are "the substitution of secondary for primary contacts, the weakening of bonds of kinship, and the declining social significance of the family, the disappearance of the neighborhood, and the undermining of the traditional basis of social solidarity." With this collapse of gemeinschaft, Wirth supposed that "competition and formal control mechanisms [would have to] furnish the substitute for the bonds of solidarity that are relied upon to hold a folk society together." Finally, he noted a "levelling influence" characteristic of urbanism. With the emergence of a common urban way of life, differences in life-styles based upon distinctive subcultures and preurban heritages (e.g., ethnic groupings) might be expected eventually to disappear.[19]

Wirth's essay is now nearly forty years old, yet no alternative theory has seriously challenged its ascendancy among students of community and urban life. Claude S. Fischer, in a recent assessment of community research in the social sciences, concludes that "Wirth's presentation remains the most explicit, seminal, and comprehensive framework for the study of Community and personality.

17. It might be noted that Wirth's first scholarly publication was a sympathetic assessment of the sociology of Ferdinand Tönnies (Wirth, "Sociology of Ferdinand Tönnies").

18. Wirth, "Urbanism as a Way of Life," in Reiss, p. 62.

19. Ibid., pp. 71, 79–80, 70, 76.

Though 'Urbanism as a Way of Life' has been extensively criticized, no other theory comprehending the nature of urban life has been advanced which is as significant, as compelling, and as consonant with both Western thought and classical sociology."[20]

———◆———

The other major contemporary theory deriving from the gemeinschaft–gesellschaft typology is identified with Talcott Parsons. His famous "pattern variables" are derived from Tönnies's formulation.[21] What Parsons did, however, was to expand Tönnies's single *Gemeinschaft–Gesellschaft* dichotomy into four parallel dichotomies:[22]

Affectivity versus affective neutrality
Particularism versus universalism
Ascription (quality) versus achievement (performance)
Diffuseness versus specificity

Parsons argues that in any situation calling for "social action" the "actor" must decide which of the two "orientations" present in each of these dichotomies is an appropriate basis for acting. For example, when greeting one's mother at a holiday reunion, an expression of affectivity may be appropriate, but when introducing oneself at the Internal Revenue Service office during a tax audit, affective neutrality may be in order. In every situation, then, the individual must decide whether his or her orientation to a particular other will be affectively neutral or not; whether to relate in terms of universalistic criteria or in terms of a particular or special relationship that may exist; whether to accept ascriptive bases of status, qualities essentially products of birth (e.g., family background or racial identifica-

20. Fischer, "Study of Urban Community," p. 72.
21. On the close association of this formulation with Tönnies's typology, see Talcott Parsons, Robert Bales, and Edward Shils, *Working Papers in the Theory of Action* (New York: Free Press, 1953), pp. 207n–208n. See also Marion Levy, Jr., *Modernization and the Structure of Societies* (Princeton: Princeton University, 1966), p. 136n.
22. In early formulations, Parsons had five dichotomies. The fifth was self-orientation versus collectivity orientation.

tion), or to accept achievement (e.g., professional certification) as the only basis of status; and, finally, whether to respond diffusely to the whole person (as to a spouse) or to that specific portion of the total person that is expressed through some specialized functional role (as to a store clerk).[23]

When Parsons explains these pattern variables, they simply define alternative orientations to social action available in every social situation. They do not suggest, as Maine's dichotomy explicitly did, anything about the direction of historical change. Yet when Parsons and his followers apply the pattern variables to the analysis of social change, the evolutionary assumptions underlying the typological approach become apparent.[24] Here the dichotomies do not stand as the characteristic dilemmas of modern society; rather, they stand as ideal types representing stages of historical evolution. All of the orientations in the left-hand column of the list of Parsons's dichotomies are identified with "traditional" or communal orientations to social action, whereas those in the right-hand column represent a modern orientation. When Parsons first devised the scheme, he was attempting to explain the distinctive role and cultural style of professionals in American society, so his studies involved him in an examination of the interplay of the two orientations within society.[25] Gradually, however, his attention shifted from considerations of individuals and groups within a society to considerations of whole societies and whether their value systems were characterized by affectivity, particularism, ascription, and diffuseness or by affective neutrality, universalism, achievement, and specificity.[26]

23. See Talcott Parsons, *The Social System* (New York: Free Press, 1951), pp. 58–77; Talcott Parsons and Edward Shils, *Toward a General Theory of Action* (New York: Harper, 1962), pp. 76–88; and Talcott Parsons, "Pattern Variables Revisited: A Response to Robert Dubin," *ASR*, 25 (1960): 467–483.

24. On this and the shift in Parsons's interests noted at the end of the paragraph, see the brief discussion in Robert Nisbet, *Social Change and History* (New York: Oxford University Press, 1969), pp. 262–266.

25. See Talcott Parsons, "The Professions and the Social Structure," *Social Forces*, 17 (1939): 466–467.

26. For reasons that should become apparent as the discussion progresses and in the following chapters, the theory is more fruitful when used to investigate specific groups or institutions within the larger society than when used in discussions of whole societies. Parsons's investigations of the family and the professions are more interesting, for example, than his more general discussions of nation-size social systems.

The increased interest in developing nations in the years following World War II encouraged Parsons and other American social scientists to use the pattern variables as indexes for comparing the relative "modernity" of developing nations.[27] These psychological traits were associated with the movement from simple to more complex and differentiated social systems. As in Wirth's theory, specific social-psychological patterns were correlated with the process of specialization and the division of labor. This process of change was explained by Parsons in terms of the functional requirements of the structure or social system itself. According to this so-called structural-functional approach, the pattern of social change can be deduced logically from the structure itself, independent of time, place, or context; independent, in short, of history.

The major theoretical fruit of this endeavor was the development of a comprehensive theory of social change based upon the traditional–modern dichotomy initially formulated by Tönnies.[28] Modernization theory, as this approach to comparative history came to be called, emerged as the dominant explanation of societal change during the 1960s. According to its logic, the progressive movement of history involved the replacement of community and communal ways (those orientations labeled by Parsons ascriptive, affective, particularistic, and diffuse) by modern ways. Historians going to the social sciences in the hope of enriching their stock of conceptual tools usually picked up one or another version of this theory. Few of these historians, however, sought to test the theory with historical materials; instead they rather mechanically inserted historical data into the framework supplied by the essentially ahistorical logic of change offered by modernization theory.[29]

27. For Parsons's emerging interest in total societies, see Parsons, *Societies: Evolutionary and Comparative Perspectives* (Englewood Cliffs, N.J.: Prentice-Hall, 1966). See also Shils, "Contemplation of Society in America," p. 407.

28. On this explicit derivation, see the statement by Levy, *Modernization and the Structure of Societies*, pp. 135–136.

29. For a recent effort to direct historians to Parsons, see Louis Galambos, "Parsonian Sociology and Post-Progressive History," *Social Science Quarterly*, 50 (1969): 25–45. Two ambitious attempts at historical synthesis based on modernization theory are Cyril E. Black, *The Dynamics of Modernization* (New York: Harper, 1967), and Richard D. Brown, *Modernization: The Transformation of American Life, 1600–1865* (New York: Hill & Wang, 1976).

In respect to community and social change, then, one finds remarkable agreement between the two dominant social theories of contemporary American social science. Both are essentially linear or evolutionary models of societal change in which community is replaced by association and formal organization. They are distinguished from one another only by the effort of urban theory to relate the shift from gemeinschaft to gesellschaft to changes in human settlement patterns, yet even here, Wirth was explicit in pointing out that the changes he associated with urbanism extended out beyond the compact city to transform the whole society.[30] This convergence of the two theories should not, perhaps, be surprising. Both theories derive from the *Gemeinschaft–Gesellschaft* distinction formulated by Tönnies. Indeed, they might plausibly be interpreted as domestic and foreign policy versions of the same sociological idea.

For all their logical coherence and rhetorical power, however, these formulations of social theory leave many social scientists uneasy. Tom Bottomore, for example, has recently pointed out that sociologists are repeatedly surprised by the continuing importance of traditional values and communal bonds among the peoples of developing nations and by the persistence of significant kinship and other primary groupings in modern urban society.[31] Gerhard Lenski's observation on the gap between theory and the survey data he collected for Detroit is typical in form as well as in content:

> What is startling about our present study is the finding that communalism survives, and even thrives, in the heart of the modern metropolis, though admittedly in a guise which makes its recognition difficult for those accustomed to associating communalism with geographically isolated and numerically small populations.[32]

30. See Wirth, "Urbanism as a Way of Life," p. 64.
31. Tom Bottomore, *Sociology: A Guide to Problems and Literature* (New York: Random House, Vintage, 1972), p. 105.
32. Gerhard Lenski, *The Religious Factor: A Sociological Study of Religion's Impact on Politics, Economy, and Family Life,* rev. ed. (Garden City, N.Y.: Doubleday, Anchor, 1963), p. 328.

The purpose of a social theory or a metaphor of social change is to provide manageable conceptual handles that bring enough order to the chaos of social experience to enable us to grasp the actual structure of society. It is evident that the most common formulations of Tönnies's theory in the middle of the twentieth century fail us in this respect. The cause of this failure is related, at least in part, to the schism that has developed between sociology and history during recent decades. These theories lack a firm attachment to the historical record of social change over the course of American history and as a result, offer a logic of history rather than a historically grounded account of social change.

Evidence, Logic, Theory

Empirical evidence contrary to Wirth's hypothesis has been building up for decades. As early as 1952, Oscar Lewis, in an article titled "Urbanization without Breakdown," reported that in his study of social life in a Mexican city he found traditional forms of solidarity persisting. He speculated, moreover, that the family might even be strengthened, or made more rather than less significant, during the urbanization process. Lewis also raised another important issue: the possibility that Wirth's theory was culture bound and thereby valid only for Western Europe and the United States. The Mexican data, according to Lewis, suggested that "urbanization is not a simple, unitary, universally similar process, but that it assumes different forms and meanings depending upon the prevailing historic, economic, social, and cultural conditions." A few years later, Richard Morse, a historian, assembled historical and sociological evidence from a broader range of Latin American societies in order to make the same point. He did not find in Latin American cities that primary relations and personalistic forms of social cohesion were being replaced by voluntary associations and rationalistic and depersonalized forms of social organization.[33]

If Wirth's theory was not a universal explanation capable of ex-

33. Oscar Lewis, "Urbanization without Breakdown," *The Scientific Monthly*, 75 (1952): 39; Richard Morse, "Latin American Cities: Aspects of Function and Structure," *CSSH*, 4 (1959): 473–493.

plaining urbanization in all cultures, was it able to describe the process accurately in the United States alone? Here, too, contradictory evidence began to emerge beginning in the 1950s. Perhaps the first important empirical challenge was Donald Foley's discovery in 1952 of "neighborly" bonds in a Rochester, New York, residential district, where, it turned out, urban life had not totally assumed the qualities that Wirth identified with urbanism.[34] Over the years, social surveys undertaken by Wendell Bell, Scott Greer, Morris Janowitz, and others revealed that social relationships that might be communal remained important even in the largest cities.[35] Eugene Litwack, Marvin Sussman, and others demonstrated that the nuclear family was neither isolated nor insignificant in modern urban life; Herbert Gans, Gerald Suttles, Joe Feagin, Carol Stack, and Marc Fried showed that ethnic, class, and racial neighborhoods persisted in the city and that primary relationships provided the social foundation for them.[36] Claude Fischer has suggested that cultural

34. Donald L. Foley, *Neighbors or Urbanites? The Study of a Rochester Residential District*, University of Rochester Studies of Metropolitan Rochester, no. 2 (Rochester, N.Y., 1952).

35. I emphasize that they *might* be communal because these scholars, although they refer to ties of community, seem to lump together a rather wide range of relationships, from casual to intimate, as evidence contrary to Wirth. Some of the relationships they have uncovered do, however, seem to fit my rather restrictive definition of community. See Wendell Bell and Marion D. Boat, "Urban Neighborhoods and Informal Social Relations," *AJS*, 62 (1957): 391–398; Scott Greer, *The Urbane View* (New York: Oxford University Press, 1972); and Morris Janowitz, *The Community Press in an Urban Setting*, 2d ed. (Chicago: University of Chicago, 1967).

36. Eugene Litwack, "Occupational Mobility and Extended Family Cohesion," *ASR*, 25 (1960): 9–21; idem., "Geographical Mobility and Extended Family Cohesion," ibid., pp. 385–394; Eugene Litwack and Ivan Szelenyi, "Primary Group Structures and Their Functions: Kin, Neighbors, and Friends," ibid., 34 (1969): 465–481; Marvin B. Sussman, "The Isolated Nuclear Family: Fact or Fiction," *Social Problems*, 6 (1959): 333–340; Marvin Sussman and Lee Burchinal, "Kin Family Network: Unheralded Structure in Current Conceptualizations of Family Functioning," *Marriage and Family Living*, 24 (1962): 231–240; Michael Young and Peter Willmott, *Family and Kinship in East London* (New York: Penguin, 1962); Bert N. Adams, "Isolation, Function, and Beyond: American Kinship in the 1960s," *Journal of Marriage and the Family*, 32 (1970): 575–597; Herbert Gans, *The Urban Villagers* (New York: Free Press, 1962); Gerald D. Suttles, *The Social Order of the Slum* (Chicago: University of Chicago, 1968); Joe R. Feagin, "The Social Ties of Negroes in an Urban Environment: Structure and Variation" (Ph.D. diss., Harvard, 1966); Carol B. Stack, *All Our Kin: Strategies for Survival in a Black Community* (New York: Harper, 1974); Marc Fried, *The World of the Urban Working Class* (Cambridge: Harvard University, 1973).

diversity and subcultural identification might be enhanced in the city. Others have revealed, as Weber had predicted, that, even in the largest bureaucracies—those most prominent symbols of urbanism—strong personal relationships between whole people can be formed.[37]

Community is apparently more pervasive than urban theory would predict. Although not all of these empirical studies agree in their definition of community, collectively they offer a formidable body of contrary evidence for Wirth's theory. Morris Janowitz and John Kasarda, in a recent survey of the empirical data available on urban life-styles, conclude that the Tönnies–Wirth model of social change might be faulted for being essentially a "reasoned moral position" rather than a plan "for empirical research," but its most serious problem is "that it fails to explain the extent and forms of community organization found in modern society."[38] Curiously, however, these empirical challenges to Wirth's theory have not produced an alternative one that more effectively orders the available empirical data. As a result, urban theory is, in the words of Claude Fischer, "at an impasse," and no one can read the growing number of criticisms of modernization theory without concluding that it, too, is at an impasse.[39]

Negative findings in empirical studies are often treated either as lingering vestiges of community that will soon disappear or as

37. Claude S. Fischer, "Toward a Subcultural Theory of Urbanism," *AJS*, 80 (1975): 1319–1341; Max Weber, *The Theory of Social and Economic Organization*, trans. Talcott Parsons (New York: Free Press, 1964), p. 137; Edward Shils, "Primordial, Personal, Sacred and Civil Ties," *British Journal of Sociology*, 8 (1957): 130–145; S. N. Eisenstadt, "The Relations between Sociological Theory and Anthropological Research," in his *Essays in Comparative Institutions* (New York: Wiley, 1965), p. 90; and George C. Homans, *The Human Group* (New York: Harcourt, 1950), pp. 150–151. In a relatively stable economy, enduring business relationships can assume communal kinds of interaction. See Wilbert E. Moore, *Social Change* (Englewood Cliffs, N.J.: Prentice-Hall, 1963), pp. 107–108.

38. John Kasarda and Morris Janowitz, "Community Sentiment in Mass Society," *ASR*, 39 (1974): 329.

39. Fischer, "Study of Urban Community," p. 73. On modernization theory, see, for example, Joseph Gusfield, "Tradition and Modernity: Misplaced Polarities in the Study of Social Change," *AJS*, 72 (1967): 351–362; Dean C. Tipps, "Modernization Theory and the Comparative Study of Societies," *CSSH*, 15 (1973): 199–226; and L. E. Shiner, "Tradition/Modernity: An Ideal Type Gone Astray," ibid., 17 (1975): 245–252.

puzzling exceptions. Even when they are taken as negative evidence bringing existing theory into question, these findings have not yet forced a reformulation of social theory. Although theories of urbanization and modernization do not connect very well to the actual processes of historical change, they remain the most pervasive theories of history available in contemporary social thought.

———◆———

How can we account for this dissociation of fact and theory? One might argue that the problem is more apparent than real. Wirth and Parsons both used versions of the ideal-type methodology developed by Max Weber. Typological constructs, Weber explained, need not perfectly reflect any existing society. Their purpose is to provide definitions, partly arbitrary, that are fruitful in investigating and theorizing about actual societies. Some empirical contradictions are therefore to be expected.[40] Even if we acknowledge this, however, a serious problem remains. The versions of the gemeinschaft–gesellschaft typology found in contemporary social theory seem to have had only marginal success in describing and explaining the actual processes of historical change associated with urbanization and modernization.

Whatever the virtues or defects of ideal-type methodologies, the problem with these theories lies elsewhere. We must look at them first as forms or logics of historical explanation. Both theories are burdened with important assumptions that give them rhetorical force, but at the cost of diverting attention from the actual processes of historical change.

The gemeinschaft–gesellschaft, rural–urban, traditional–modern dichotomies are used, as I have already noted, to characterize whole societies. Change is perceived in totalistic terms: A society is either modern or traditional, urban or rural. This change, moreover, is sequential. One kind of society succeeds another, and this pattern of change is viewed through lenses that have a progressivist tint. Evolution from one pole to the other is seen as reflecting the pro-

40. See Weber, *Theory of Social and Economic Organization*, pp. 109–112.

gressive direction of history. Within these linear models, movement is not only directional, but is usually treated as unilinear, with all urban and modern societies converging as a single societal type where gemeinschaft is replaced by gesellschaft. Most important of all, perhaps, the urbanization and modernization process is treated as a zero-sum equation, which is to say that any growth in gesellschaft requires an equivalent diminution of gemeinschaft until ultimately the society under study is completely transformed.[41]

Although the substance of this formulation is new and distinctive to American social theory in the mid-twentieth century, as a form of historical explanation, it is old.[42] It is similar to what J. H. Hexter, in a classic historiographical essay, found in A. F. Pollard's *Factors in Modern History* (1907). It may be easier to understand the problems with contemporary theory if we begin with this distant example. Hexter isolated two underlying assumptions in Pollard's book that, he argues, actually diverted Pollard from historical research. One was the book's progressivist or evolutionary assumption; the other was what Hexter called the law of the "conservation of historical energy."

History, Pollard assumed, moved in a straight line toward the present. If the middle class was significant in Victorian England but not in the tenth century, then the intervening centuries of history could be written in terms of the "rise of the middle class." Given his commitment to evolutionary theory, what better way to connect the tenth and nineteenth centuries than with a straight line showing the progressive ascendancy of the middle class? "In fact," Hexter points out, "there is no reason to assume that the slopes or the curves of ascent of the middle class . . . during more than half a millennium were straight lines, or even that they trended continuously upward over their whole course." The task of the historian is precisely to

41. For discussions of this point in respect to urban and modernization theory, see, respectively, Gerald D. Suttles, *The Social Construction of Communities* (Chicago: University of Chicago, 1972), p. 258; and Shiner, "Tradition/Modernity," p. 252.

42. Robert Nisbet has traced the basic idea back to the origins of Western thought. For his critique, see his *Social Change and History* and *The Social Bond* (New York: Random House, 1970), chaps. 13–14.

develop empirical methods for determining the changing fate of the middle class. Pollard, however, "was not aware that his views involved any empirical problem of measurement." The straight line was, Hexter observes, "wholly *a priori*, a purely imaginary construction that does not set historical facts in order, but altogether escapes and soars above their dreary restrictions."[43]

The assumption of the conservation of historical energy relates to the way Pollard and other historians and social scientists use dichotomies to explain social change. Hexter states the idea abstractly and then provides an example: "The idea is that in a given society the energy expended on a single pair of polar elements is fixed, so that any flow of social energy in the direction of one such pole can only take place by way of subtraction from the flow of energy to the opposite pole."[44] Hexter offers Pollard's treatment of religion and secularism in the sixteenth century as an example: When Pollard found an increase of secular activity, he assumed that there must have been a corresponding decrease in its opposite, religious activity. Although this may have been true, to assume it is true is to fall into an intellectual trap. The logic of this form of historical explanation encouraged Pollard to overlook, or explain away, empirical evidence of significant religious activity in the sixteenth century. Whatever the logic of polar dichotomies, there is no reason why the historical record might not show a simultaneous increase in such opposites as secularism and religion.

Just as the underlying logic in Pollard's chosen forms of historical explanation obscured the actual historical record of religious activity in the sixteenth century, so the narrative structure one finds in contemporary formulations of the gemeinschaft–gesellschaft distinction diverts attention from the actual place of community in modern urban society. The assumptions that underlie contemporary applications of the gemeinschaft–gesellschaft notion must be examined as Hexter examined Pollard's assumptions. Is it empirically true that the relation of gemeinschaft and gesellschaft is sequential?

43. J. H. Hexter, *Reappraisals in History* (New York: Harper, 1963), p. 39.
44. Ibid., p. 40.

Is change along this continuum (or dichotomy) uniform and total? Is change really unilinear and unidirectional, as most formulations imply?

To escape the constraints of the gemeinschaft–gesellschaft logic, what we need is a notion of differential change.[45] Perhaps certain modern social developments might even reenforce or invigorate other traditional patterns of social relations in the same society.[46] Why cannot gemeinschaft and gesellschaft simultaneously shape social life? Why must we assume that there is a single direction of change in a single society, or in a single social process? Recent research on urbanization suggests that there is no uniform direction in the effects of urbanism on patterns of cultural life. It does not necessarily spawn secular, rationalistic values and behavior. Indeed, it appears that in some cases urbanization can actually increase ethnic identification and what sociologists call "primordial ties."[47]

The Amish in the United States provide an illuminating example of differential social change. Living within the most modern and urbanized of societies, they continue their intense religious communalism. In his excellent study of the Amish, John Hostetler concludes that their history has important implications for general social theory. Social change among the Amish, he writes, "does not necessarily proceed from the simple to the complex, nor do all societies go through certain presumed stages in the social evolutionary process. Changes in Amish society are not predestined to proceed from the sacred to the secular. . . . Not only have we found in our

45. This argument is made by Clifford Geertz in *Peddlers and Princes: Social Change and Economic Modernization in Two Indonesian Towns* (Chicago: University of Chicago, 1963), pp. 143–153. See also Daniel Rodgers, "Tradition, Modernity, and the American Industrial Worker: Reflections and Critique," *JIH*, 7 (1977): 655–681; and Brown, *Modernization*.

46. See, for example, Charles P. Loomis and Olen Leonard, *Culture of a Contemporary Rural Community: El Cerrito, New Mexico* (Washington, D.C.: U.S. Department of Agriculture, 1941). See also Tipps, "Modernization Theory and the Comparative Study of Societies," p. 215; Gusfield, "Tradition and Modernity," p. 20; and Kai T. Erikson, *Everything in Its Path: Destruction of Community in the Buffalo Creek Flood* (New York: Simon & Schuster, 1976), pt. II.

47. See Fischer, "Toward a Subcultural Theory of Urbanism," p. 1335. See also Shils, "Primordial, Personal, Sacred and Civil Ties," p. 131.

observations a number of instances of secularization, but also the process of becoming more and more sacred."[48] Some Amish, for example, adhere to stricter religious regulations now than one hundred years ago. It would be a mistake, then, to assume that all change stimulated by interaction of a small community with larger society is in the direction of conformity to the external world.[49]

Scholars wrestling with the contradictions emerging from the application of urbanization and modernization theories to nonwestern societies are beginning to question their earlier unidirectional and unilinear assumptions. Brian J. L. Berry, a geographer deeply involved with the development of urban policy, has recently recanted his former beliefs. He no longer accepts the "conventional wisdom" that urbanization is a "universal process, a consequence of modernisation that involves the same sequence of events in different countries and that produces a progressive convergence of forms." He also rejects the view that "there may be several culturally specific processes, but that they are producing convergent results because of underlying technological imperatives of modernisation and industrialisation."[50] Modernization theorist S. N. Eisenstadt has moved in a similar direction in his recent work. He stresses the "historical dimension" of modernization and denies that it is a universal process with its own logic. He also denies that there is a convergence of societies or a fixed plateau toward which progressive societies are moving.[51] The fate of community, in other words, might well be decided by specific historical circumstances rather than by the inexorable logic of urbanization and modernization.

The Double Heritage of Tönnies

However critical I have been of urban and modernization theory, I am not proposing that we abandon theory and concentrate entirely

48. John A. Hostetler, *Amish Society* (Baltimore: Johns Hopkins, 1963), p. 307.
49. Ibid., p. 294. Canadian Mennonites similarly preserved communalism in the city. See Leo Drieger, "Canadian Mennonite Urbanism: Ethnic Villages or Metropolitan Remnant?" *The Mennonite Quarterly Review*, 49 (1975): 226–241.
50. Berry, *Human Consequences of Urbanisation*, p. xii.
51. S. N. Eisenstadt, *Tradition, Change and Modernity* (New York: Wiley, 1973), p. 358.

upon the concrete and particular. Rather, we must strive to cast our theory in terms that can accommodate the concreteness of context and the particularity of change over time, and I propose that the theoretical tradition we have been considering is easily adapted to such historical reconstruction. Most current formulations of Tönnies's theory overlook an exciting potential for historical scholarship and for a richer understanding of community and social change that the initial formulation of the theory contained but that has been given insufficient attention by sociologists and historians of community.

Simply placing Tönnies and his development of the *Gemeinschaft–Gesellschaft* typology into proper historical context begins to reveal the real meaning of his concept and its usefulness for the study of community. Tönnies wrote at a time when the small towns of Germany and the people from them who valued small-town patterns of community were being integrated into larger structures of society that had emerged with the growth of cities, industrial capitalism, and the centralized national state.[52] Tönnies formulated his *Gemeinschaft–Gesellschaft* distinction at a time when men and women were intensely conscious of being involved in two kinds of human interaction. His terms *Gemeinschaft* and *Gesellschaft* described these two patterns of social relations that coexisted in everyone's social experience. *Gemeinschaft* and *Gesellschaft* were not places; they were forms of human interaction.

These two kinds of interaction constituted the social alternatives available in modern society. Moreover, he anticipated that both of these forms of interaction were likely to be permanent aspects of all social life. Whereas he indicated that *Gesellschaft* was gaining significance in people's lives, he did not say that *all* relationships were or would become what he called *Gesellschaft*. "The force of Gemeinschaft persists," he wrote, "even within the period of Gesellschaft."[53] Tönnies, in other words, used his dichotomy in two

52. For the social background of German social philosophy, see the brilliant book by Mack Walker, *German Home Towns: Community, State and General Estate* (Ithaca, N.Y.: Cornell University, 1971).

53. Tönnies, *Community and Society*, p. 232. In fairness to those who have read Tönnies differently than I read him, it must be acknowledged that he is occasionally

ways: to denote the character of a whole society in a particular historical period and to describe two patterns of human relationships within that society.[54]

This second aspect of Tönnies's theory has never been entirely neglected by students of community, but neither has its potential been fully exploited to develop a complex understanding of the process of social change within a single society. If the first aspect of Tönnies's theory is liable to lead to ahistorical or purely logical depictions of the shift from community to association as the basis of society, his second point suggests the possibility of a rigorous empirical account of the changing structure and meaning of community over time. The recovery of this dual aspect of Tönnies's theory offers an analytical concept for examining the social processes involved in the emergence of modern society.

Other social theorists of Tönnies's generation had the same dualistic conceptions of the ideal-type dichotomies they and Tönnies developed. Weber, for example, used Tönnies's terms to designate different "interactive tendencies" within single societies rather than to describe whole societal types. Durkheim, who apparently developed his concepts of "mechanical" and "organic" solidarity independent of Tönnies, similarly believed that modern society contained both of them simultaneously. He perceived the advent of organic solidarity as Tönnies viewed the emergence of *Gesellschaft*: it was a historical event in modern society that produced two closely interrelated but distinct patterns of social interac-

---

contradictory on this point. Compare the following statement: "But as the town lives on within the city, elements of life in the Gemeinschaft, as the only real form of life, persist within the Gesellschaft, although lingering and decaying. . . . On the other hand, the more general the condition Gesellschaft becomes in the nation or a group of nations, the more this entire 'country' or the entire 'world' begins to resemble one large city" (ibid., p. 227). See also ibid., p. 198 (addendum written in 1912).

54. This point, ignored by most commentators, is noted with exceptional clarity by Bottomore, *Sociology*, pp. 100–101. In his work on the family and the professions, Parsons seems to use his pattern variables in a way that is sensitive to this complexity of social interaction, but this is not the case when he talks about total societies. See especially Talcott Parsons and Robert Bales, *Family, Socialization and Interaction* (New York: Free Press, 1953), pp. 11–12, 19; Parsons, "Professions and the Social Structure," pp. 466–467.

tion. These "two societies," Durkheim wrote, "really make up only one. They are two aspects of one and the same reality, but none the less they must be distinguished." If Tönnies noted that the town lives within the city, Durkheim believed that "there is a social life outside of the whole division of labor, but which the latter presupposes."[55]

In the United States, Edward A. Ross, one of the Progressive era's most influential social theorists, rejected (or failed to see) Tönnies's dualistic notion and offered a linear model of change that anticipated Wirth and the modernization theorists. In *Social Control* (1901), his most important book, Ross argued that "powerful forces are more and more transforming *community* into *society,* that is, replacing living tissue with structures held together by rivets and screws." He informed his readers in a footnote that this community –society contrast was similar to that made by Tönnies in *Gemeinschaft und Gesellschaft,* but he insisted that he had formulated his own idea before he became acquainted with the work of Tönnies. Whether he actually borrowed the notion from Tönnies is less important than the difference between the two men's theories. We find in Ross no sense of communal and associational patterns of social relations coexisting in modern society. He offers instead an early version of the community breakdown theory that culminates in Wirth's essay on urbanism. For social theorists concerned about social order, Ross's interpretation of social change had important public-policy implications that are clear in the book's title, *Social Control.* With the erosion of all traditional or communal forms of social cohesion in modern urban society, it was essential, Ross argued, to develop artificial or formal institutional mechanisms of social control.[56]

Much of the concern for social control that historians have found in their studies of Progressive reformers stems from such interpreta-

---

55. Max Weber, *The City,* trans. Don Martindale and Gertrude Neuwirth (New York: Free Press, 1958), p. 106n; Durkheim, *Division of Labor in Society,* pp. 129, 277. See also ibid., pp. 227–229.

56. Edward A. Ross, *Social Control: A Survey of the Foundations of Order* (Cleveland: Case Western Reserve University, 1969), p. 432.

tions of modern society. Beyond the obvious concern for social control, this notion has an important, if not immediately apparent, political aspect. It implicitly denies legitimacy to particularistic sources of political power based upon sentiment and upon such solidarity groups as neighborhood, ethnic cultures, or even class. The only legitimate political allegiance was to the abstract and rationalistic notion that replaced the old experiential community: the public interest.[57]

If in American social science there was a clear tradition extending from Ross to Wirth that emphasized one aspect of Tönnies's theory and denied or de-emphasized the other, there was also an important group of Progressive social theorists who maintained the dual perspective of Tönnies. Although acknowledging that the advent of modern, urban society meant more gesellschaft, they agreed with Tönnies and Durkheim that community was still vital. The obvious diminution of the extent of community in modern society seemed to require less attention than the interplay and interrelations between remaining contexts of community and larger structures of society. These communitarian social thinkers include Charles Horton Cooley, Jane Addams, Robert Park, Mary Parker Follett, and John Dewey.[58]

Cooley, for example, believed that, even in modern cities, primary

57. See Michael H. Frisch, "Social Particularity and American Political Culture: The Two Edged Sword of Community," in *The City and Sense of Community*, ed. Sander Gilman (Ithaca, N.Y.: Center for Urban Development Research, 1976), pp. 32–37. The work of Samuel P. Hays has shown how particularistic sources of political power were eroded by the advent of broader notions of the social order or the public interest. See his "The Politics of Reform in Municipal Government in the Progressive Era," *Pacific Northwest Quarterly*, 55 (1964): 157–169; idem., "Political Parties and the Community–Society Continuum," in *The American Party Systems: Stages of Political Development*, ed. William N. Chambers and Walter D. Burnham (New York: Oxford University Press, 1967), pp. 152–181.

58. See David E. Price, "Community and Control: Critical Democratic Theory in the Progressive Period," *APSR*, 68 (1974): 1663–1678. See also Jean B. Quandt, *From the Small Town to the Great Community: The Social Thought of Progressive Intellectuals* (New Brunswick, N.J.: Rutgers University, 1970), for, although it is a sustained attack on communitarian thought from a position that sees community as anachronistic or incompatible with the "functional organization" of modern society (p. 158), it nonetheless contains much useful material on Addams, Cooley, Dewey, Follett, and Park.

relations provided the context for everyone's first social experience and for the shaping of everyone's social consciousness; the "more elaborate relations" of the larger society were formed on the foundation of primary relations. In his study of social organization, Cooley reflected on the prospects of primary groups in the city: "In our own cities the crowded tenements and the general economic and social confusion have sorely wounded the family and the neighborhood, but it is remarkable, in view of these conditions, what vitality they show; and there is nothing upon which the conscience of the time is more determined than upon restoring them to health." He also believed that such a reinvigoration of informal and intimate groups in the city would involve "trusting democracy more rather than less."[59]

This social and political task was embraced by Jane Addams, who sought, through the settlement house she established in Chicago, to enhance democracy while making the local neighborhood a community within the city. Mary Parker Follett of Boston theorized about the necessity of revitalizing the neighborhood as a social and political group that might counterbalance the modern tendency toward bureaucratization and centralization.[60] Both social forms existed; both had their positive uses.

Robert Park is especially interesting because he was Wirth's teacher at the University of Chicago. It is illuminating to contrast Park's classic essay on the city with Wirth's. In "The City: Suggestions for the Investigation of Human Behavior in the City Environment," published in 1915, Park presented a complex mosaic of social forms and patterns of social interaction in the city that stands in sharp contrast to Wirth's stark portrayal of relentless movement from community to association in the modern city. Park accepted the notion that urbanization brought with it an increase in gesellschaft and a reliance upon "positive law," but he was also intrigued

59. Cooley, *Social Organization*, pp. 26–27; idem. *Social Process* (New York: Scribner's, 1918), p. 149.
60. For Addams's notion of community in the modern city, see her *Twenty Years at Hull House* (New York: Macmillan, 1910; New York: New American Library, Signet, 1961); for Follett, see her book *The New State*.

by the diversity of social worlds that continued to exist and inter-
penetrate, each of them small communities or "moral regions"
within the larger city. In its sensitivity to the coexistence of both
gemeinschaft and gesellschaft in the city, Park's urban thought was
"double visioned."[61] It was not one type replacing another; it was
each individual being involved in alternate forms of human interaction.

With this perception of urban social patterns, it might have been
possible to reorient urban research to focus on the interplay of
different patterns of social groupings rather than simply to record
the decay predicted by the linear model, yet Park never developed
this notion. During the 1920s, his interests shifted toward human
ecology, and by the 1930s, he seems to have abandoned his earlier
concern for community in the city.[62]

In the late 1920s, John Dewey made his strongest plea for revitalizing community in modern society. Denying the existence of any
inevitable evolution of society from individualism to collectivity or
any other social form, Dewey insisted that social change "has con-
sisted in a continuous redistribution of social integrations." He as-
serted that "there is nothing intrinsic in the forces which have
effected uniform standardization, mobility, and remote invisible relationships that is fatally obstructive to the return movement of
their consequences into the local homes of mankind."[63]

Modern life, by drawing people into larger associations, freed
them, Dewey maintained, from the constriction of the traditional
small town, yet within this larger society, he insisted, the small
community remains vital. If parochial communities are prone to

61. Robert Park, "The City: Suggestions for the Investigation of Human Behavior
in the City Environment," *AJS,* 20 (1915): 593–600. The phrase "double visioned" is
from Park Dixon Goist, "City and 'Community': The Urban Theory of Robert Park,"
AQ, 23 (1971): 47.
62. See Quandt, *From the Small Town to the Great Community,* pp. 153–154. One
can see the beginnings of this shift by comparing the revisions Park made in his 1915
essay on the city when he republished it in 1925. Cf. "The City: Suggestions for the
Investigation of Human Behavior in the Urban Environment," in *The City,* Robert
Park and Ernest W. Burgess (Chicago: University of Chicago, 1967), pp. 1–46.
63. John Dewey, *The Public and Its Problems* (New York: Holt, 1927), pp. 193,
215.

deadness and intellectual stagnation, the intrusion of the larger society's institutions promise a "variegated and many-hued experience." Community and society, in their creative interplay, provide the basis for a more intelligent and effective democracy. "In its deepest and richest sense," Dewey observed, "a community must always remain a matter of face-to-face intercourse. . . . The Great Community, in the sense of free and full intercommunication, is conceivable. But it can never possess all the qualities which mark a local community. It will do its final work in ordering the relations and enriching the experience of local associations." Expressing his hopes for America, he concluded: "Whatever the future may have in store, one thing is certain. Unless local communal life can be restored, the public cannot adequately resolve its most urgent problem: to find and identify itself."[64]

The double focus of Tönnies's sociology persisted into the 1930s. Carle Zimmerman, in discussing the tasks of community sociology in his textbook, *The Changing Community* (1938), gave both aspects of Tönnies's theory their due.[65] In the same year, however, Louis Wirth published "Urbanism as a Way of Life." In this article, called by one scholar "maybe the most influential article ever to appear in a sociological journal,"[66] Wirth emphasized the first aspect of Tönnies's formulation to the practical exclusion of the second. With the dualistic perspective of Tönnies largely submerged in Wirth's evolutionary formulation, a complex theory with rich possibilities for historical research was transformed into a simplistic typology of social change. Indeed, the complexities that remained in Wirth's statement were typically ignored in the brief summaries of it that appeared when it was cited later in sociological journals.

It is difficult to determine why one aspect of Tönnies's theory was so de-emphasized by most sociologists after World War II. One possibility, of course, is that Wirth expressed his theory with such

64. Ibid., pp. 216, 211, 216.
65. Zimmerman, *Changing Community*. The theme runs through the whole book, but see pp. 83, 114.
66. R. L. Simpson, "Sociology of the Community: Current Status and Prospects," *RS*, 30 (1965). 133.

stunning elegance that he drove out all competition, yet I expect that this is only a partial explanation that does not account for later simplifications. The historical setting for Wirth's essay suggests reasons both for its reception and for the summaries of it in the sociological literature that made it even more unilinear than it actually was: Wirth's theory entered American social science at a time when Americans were beset by tensions in domestic life and in international affairs.

Like Ross's earlier formulation, Wirth's theory of community breakdown was supportive of "liberal" efforts to achieve order and unity in social and political life. Particularistic bases of political or social action, whether based on ethnicity, class, or locality, were interpreted as nostalgic, irrelevant, and logically destined to disappear.[67] For men and women with fresh memories of Hitler's perversion of community, with numerous indications of racial and labor-union unrest in the United States, and with exaggerated fears of domestic subversion and international Communism, a vision of unilinear and inevitable progress toward a rationalized and homogenized world might have been encouraging, even if it was tinged with nostalgia for the vanishing community.

These speculations gain added weight by the coincidence that modernization theory, the foreign policy version of Wirth's theory, was developed during these same years. Here the public-policy goal was explicit: The intention was to facilitate the "development" of Third-World nations in ways that would avoid the sort of political instability that might strengthen the Communist World at the expense of the Free World.

Recovery and Reformulation

Whatever the reasons for the transformations of Tönnies's theory after World War II, most literature in the social sciences described a great change that fatally wounded community and gave birth to

67. Recall that it was during this period that Daniel Bell formulated his famous notion that ideology was irrelevant in modern society. See Daniel Bell, *The End of Ideology*, rev. ed. (New York: Free Press, 1962).

modern society. Although such analysis was obviously correct in the broadest sense, it lacked historical specificity and, by being so global, left little for historians to investigate within its terms. A notable exception, however, is the work of Robert Redfield, who did his graduate work at Chicago with Park and later taught there with Park and Wirth. He began his career with an orientation similar to Wirth's, but in the course of time, he reached beyond (or behind) Wirth to recover Tönnies's original usage of the Gemeinschaft–Gesellschaft distinction.

Redfield's intellectual journey is in itself interesting. His initial formulation of the urban–folk continuum was based on field research first undertaken at Tepoztlán, Mexico, in 1926. After publishing an ethnographic account of his findings, he used his data to formulate a very tentative and preliminary version of the folk–urban continuum, which he published in 1934. In 1941, after extensive field work in four settlements in Mexico that stood at different points on his continuum, he offered a fully developed version of his theory in the last chapter of The Folk Culture of Yucatan. His conception of the urban–folk typology derived, he wrote, from his reading of Maine, Durkheim, and, especially, Tönnies.[68] It was basically a linear model similar to Wirth's theory of urbanization, stressing the harmony of the preurban community and the breakdown of community under the impact of urbanization.

In the early 1950s, however, Oscar Lewis restudied Tepoztlán, the community where Redfield had first developed his ideas on folk and urban cultures.[69] The evidence that Lewis presented challenged both the beginning and the end point of Redfield's analysis. Lewis denied that the preurban community was nearly so isolated or so well integrated as Redfield had indicated, and he did not find the breakdown after urbanization that was predicted by both

68. Robert Redfield, Tepoztlan: A Mexican Village (Chicago: University of Chicago, 1930); idem., "Culture Change in Yucatan, AA, 36 (1934): 57–59; idem., Folk Culture of Yucatan. On this borrowing, see ibid., p. x.

69. Oscar Lewis, Life in a Mexican Village: Tepoztlán Restudied (Urbana: University of Illinois, 1951): idem., "Tepoztlán Restudied: A Critique of the Folk-Urban Conceptualization of Change," RS, 18 (1953): 121–134.

Wirth's and Redfield's theories. Redfield's response to Lewis's criticism was impressive. He did not ignore Lewis, nor did he claim that he was right and Lewis wrong. Neither, incidentally, did he admit, as Lewis suggested he ought, that he himself was wrong, misled by his own antiurban bias. Instead he attempted to rework the theoretical framework so that it might better explain both his own and Lewis's empirical findings. The result was a more complex and interesting theory.

In his reformulation, Redfield retained the general notion of sequential change that was associated with the process of urbanization, but he now speculated that folk and urban ways coexisted in the same society. Tönnies, Redfield now realized, "conceived of two imaginably distinct and contrasting aspects of all societies." He and Lewis, each with his own bias, had stressed one of the two dimensions of all social entities. Hence their work was not so much contradictory as it was complementary.[70]

Extending his new formulation, Redfield turned from Lewis's work to Helen and Robert Lynd's study of Muncie, Indiana in the 1920s. Comparing his own study of Chan Kom, a Mexican village, with the Muncie data, he observed that folk ways and urban ways were apparent in both. They are "both present in important degrees and in an interpenetration that demands analysis." The question of community required more than observation of the undeviating decline of community according to the law of the conservation of historical energy. Instead it became a task of empirically assessing the nature of the interpenetration of community and society in particular places at particular times. The student of community, Redfield suggested, needs "two lenses for seeing a compound reality." He proposed that the anthropologist (or historian) of community think of Middletown or any other local society "as an interpenetration of two opposite kinds of living, thinking, and feeling" that are simultaneously analyzable in two ways: as "an isolated, homogeneous, sacred, and personal community . . . and . . . as . . . the

70. Redfield, *The Little Community* (Chicago: University of Chicago, 1955), pp. 141–142. Cf. Rene König, *The Community* (London: Routledge & Kegan Paul, 1968), pp. 128–129.

heterogeneous, secular, and impersonal community that we find approximated in cities."[71]

From this perspective, community is not a specific space or a mere base line for historical change; it is a fundamental and enduring form of social interaction. Thinking of gemeinschaft and gesellschaft in terms of sequence is thus erroneous. They represent instead "two kinds of human collective living" in which all individuals are involved. The focus of analytical interest becomes, therefore, the interaction and interplay of communal and noncommunal ways in the lives of all.[72] Redfield's theoretical breakthrough thus offers what is, to me, precisely the vantage needed for fruitful research on community in American history.

Instead of a continuum or a sequential theory, historians seeking interesting and empirically answerable questions need a contending theory of the relation of community and society. The task of the cultural historian or critic is not to date the moment when one of the worlds of social relations is replaced by the other; it is to probe their interaction and to assess their relative salience to people's lives in specific situations. This approach makes it both easier to recognize changes in salience toward either pole of the continuum and logically possible to accept them. What we need is a perspective that will enable us to take an overview of the simultaneous polarity and reciprocity of these two patterns of human interaction. When we do this, the conceptual framework we use to guide our research will no longer supply a priori answers to the relevant historical questions. Questions of time, place, pattern, interplay, and significance will invite historical inquiry. The way will be open to empirical measurement and historical assessment of the interaction of community and society in American history.

71. Redfield, ibid., pp. 146–147.
72. Ibid., p. 147.

Chapter Three

Community in American History

When we look for community in our own time, it is often through the lenses supplied by Wirth rather than the bifocals offered by Redfield. The same is largely true of our vision of the past. It is not that the Wirthian approach is wrong, but that it is incomplete or partial. This incompleteness, often combined with unstated evolutionary assumptions, encourages a logic that avoids historical analysis—even within the discipline of history.[1] By shifting our emphasis away from the Tönnies–Wirth tradition of community theory to the Tönnies–Redfield tradition, however, we can achieve a vantage for useful historiographical criticism and for the exploration of the changing configuration of community in American history.

Community in American Historiography

A common pattern of historical explanation unites a diverse group of significant books on American history. All are sociologically informed and all reveal an acute sensitivity to the problem of community, whatever their ostensible topic. This recent historiography also shares what I will call a narrative form that is remarkably

1. Michael Zuckerman has recently called this problem an "advancing embarrassment" in his article "The Fabrication of Identity in Early America," *WMQ*, 34 (1977): 183.

similar to what one finds in Wirthian formulations of social theory. The narrative is shaped by the notion of unrelenting community decline. These works are, therefore, troubling: What is casually assumed in them to be a proper narrative structure is based upon an unexamined sociological idea.

The sociological formulation criticized in the previous chapter seems to have been absorbed into the working assumptions of historians. At a fairly deep level of consciousness, it has often provided an a priori interpretive framework for their scholarship. The process of cultural seepage that brought this sociological theory to the center of American historical writing is of great interest for modern American intellectual history. One may debate whether it entered the rhetoric of history through the explicit interdisciplinary efforts of historians, or whether it is a validation of C. Wright Mills's claim in 1959 that sociological thought had become the "common denominator of our cultural life."[2] Whatever the precise nature of this cultural diffusion, much contemporary historiography is shaped by a conceptual framework that brings history perilously close to the chasm into which ahistorical social science has already fallen.

The community breakdown model provides the structure for a series of important monographs treating different periods of American history from the seventeenth century to the twentieth. While each book is reasonably persuasive in its own terms, a problem arises when all are arranged in chronological order. Collectively, they portray the collapse of community during the lives of several successive generations of Americans. One is impelled to ask: Which study accurately captures the moment of collapse? How many times can community collapse in America? Such criticism may seem unfair. The various authors, after all, never intended their books to be laid side by side. The community decline motif, one might argue, merely represents a literary device. Perhaps, but literary devices are more important than such a defense allows.

The theme of community decline is, I acknowledge, often a liter-

2. C. Wright Mills, *The Sociological Imagination* (New York: Oxford University Press, 1959), p. 14.

ary strategy that supplies dramatic structure for these accounts of social and cultural change in America. But such structures convey analytical judgments, intended or not, that profoundly affect our understanding of the past. To say that the notion of community decline provides the dramatic structure for a work of history is to say a great deal. This structure contains and expresses a historical work's most important idea—the theory that shapes the ordering of historical evidence and that gives us our deepest sense of the past. The rhetoric of history, including strategies of persuasion, is not mere decoration; it is, as J. H. Hexter has recently argued, fundamental to historical understanding.[3] If rhetoric and structure are central to what history is all about, not only is criticism on the order I have proposed here legitimate, but it is an essential aspect of the historian's craft.

———————◆———————

It would be too unwieldly and perhaps pointless to provide a complete list of the books that share the characteristics I have just described, nor is it possible to discuss them in the detail they individually and intrinsically deserve. I can, however, illustrate my point with a brief mention of those generally acknowledged as significant in shaping our image of the American past. These studies include the work of some of the most notable historians writing today: Darrett Rutman, Bernard Bailyn, Richard Bushman, Gordon Wood, Oscar Handlin, Stephan Thernstrom, Marvin Meyers, Michael B. Katz, David Donald, Stanley Elkins, Robert Wiebe, Rowland Berthoff, and Michael Frisch. Although all of these scholars differ in their approach to history and in their perspective on the American past, the work of all of them reveals one or another version of community breakdown.

Breakdown first comes on American soil in Darrett Rutman's portrait of John Winthrop's Boston. By 1650, he argues, the communal

3. J. H. Hexter, *Doing History* (Bloomington: Indiana University, 1971), chap. 2. See also Hayden White, *Metahistory: The Historical Imagination in Nineteenth-Century Europe* (Baltimore: Johns Hopkins, 1973).

ideal articulated by Winthrop in his speech "The Model of Christian Charity" had given way to individualism, materialism, a clear distinction between sacred and secular, and associational patterns of society. "In Winthrop's Boston," he writes, "the ideal of the medieval community was transformed into the reality of modern society."[4]

Whereas Rutman sees rapid and almost total modernizing change by the middle of the seventeenth century, Bernard Bailyn offers a subtle analysis of change over a longer period in his study, *The New England Merchants in the Seventeenth Century*. In this interpretation, as well as in his companion study of Virginia elites, the crucial change occurs toward the end of the seventeenth century. Although these works draw heavily upon social science theory, they remain sensitive to particularity of time and place. They are not dependent upon an a priori logic divorced from historical actuality, nor do they suggest any kind of total shift to modernity. *The New England Merchants in the Seventeenth Century* finds its structure in empirical data and in a cultural context first mapped by Perry Miller.[5] Another of Bailyn's books on colonial American history, however— his imaginative, provocative, and influential study of education— derives, in an almost direct and mechanical way, from the sociological theory of community breakdown. The book is structured around the shift, completed in the eighteenth century, from a "homogeneous, integrated society" to one marked by "jarring multiplicity" and a "typical American individualism, optimism, and enterprise."[6]

This logic finds renewed expression in the work of some of Bailyn's best students. Richard Bushman's work on culture and society in colonial Connecticut is shaped by it, though for him the

4. Darrett B. Rutman, *Winthrop's Boston* (Chapel Hill: University of North Carolina, 1965), pp. 278–279.

5. Bernard Bailyn, *The New England Merchants in the Seventeenth Century* (New York: Harper, 1964); idem., "Politics and Social Structure in Virginia," in *Seventeenth-Century America*, ed. James Morton Smith (Chapel Hill; University of North Carolina, 1959), pp. 90–115; Perry Miller, "Declension in a Bible Commonwealth," *Proceedings of the American Antiquarian Society*, 51 (1941): 37–94.

6. Bernard Bailyn, *Education in the Forming of American Society* (New York: Random House Vintage, 1960), pp. 48–49.

great change comes later in the eighteenth century, particularly in the era of the Great Awakening. During the first half of the eighteenth century, society evolved, he argues, from a "close-knit, tightly controlled, homogeneous community" to a "new social order" that was "more open and heterogeneous." For Gordon Wood, however, the revolutionary era stands as the moment of community collapse. In *The Creation of the American Republic,* the most ambitious and compelling recent study of revolutionary politics and political theory, Wood treats republicanism as a revitalization movement seeking to restore the traditional community. Instead, however, the Revolution propelled Americans into modernity. The key shift in politics, deriving from the "social disarrangement" of the critical period, was toward a new conception of community, institutionalized in the Constitution, that was not dependent upon the organic, unified society that had by then collapsed.[7]

The pattern of successive breakdowns continues into nineteenth-century historiography. Urban studies by Oscar Handlin, Stephan Thernstrom, and Roger Lane all depend upon the breakdown thesis for their structure. Handlin's study of Boston's immigrants and Lane's study of Boston's police both begin with an organic Federalist city. Over the course of the nineteenth century, this homogeneous, unified, and stable community is disrupted by urbanization, immigration, and industrialization. The result is the development of new associational and bureaucratic (as opposed to communal) mechanisms for conducting social life and for ensuring social order.[8] The same pattern and timing is evident in Thernstrom's highly and justly praised study of Newburyport. Federalist Newburyport, he writes, was "intergrated on an almost medieval pat-

7. Richard L. Bushman, *From Puritan to Yankee: Character and the Social Order in Connecticut, 1690–1765* (New York: Norton, 1970), [p. iv]; Gordon S. Wood, *The Creation of the American Republic* (Chapel Hill: University of North Carolina, 1969), p. 474.

8. Oscar Handlin, *Boston's Immigrants,* rev. ed. (New York: Atheneum, 1959); Roger Lane, *Policing the City: Boston, 1822–1885* (New York: Atheneum, 1967). See also Oscar and Mary Handlin, *Commonwealth: A Study of the Role of Government in the American Economy, Massachusetts, 1774–1861* (New York: New York University, 1947), and idem., *The Dimensions of Liberty* (New York: Atheneum, 1966).

tern" that broke down by the 1840s "when industrialization and sudden urban growth drastically altered the composition of the Newburyport population and the relationship between the community's social groups."[9]

Other nineteenth-century studies look to the supposed collapse of community in order to explain innovative political behavior or social policy. Marvin Meyers's interpretation of the Jacksonian persuasion, for example, does not study community life, but it assumes that the breakdown of traditional values and patterns of community life explain the peculiar qualities of political rhetoric and behavior in the age of Jackson. Similarly, David Rothman assumes that the destruction of community during the same period can explain the advent of asylums, and Michael B. Katz uses community collapse to explain in part the pattern of educational reform in the middle of the nineteenth century.[10]

The historiography of the Civil War and of the Progressive movement have also been affected by this logic. David Donald and Stanley Elkins suggest that community breakdown and "social atomization" may account for the inability of Americans to develop "reasoned" solutions to the crisis of union.[11] Robert Wiebe, in *The Search for Order,* perhaps the most influential book published in the past decade, has found an explanation for Progressivism in yet another version of the community breakdown thesis. Between 1880 and 1900, he argues, the United States moved from a society based upon "island communities" characterized by autonomy, informality, and face-to-face relations to a centralized, formalized national soci-

9. Stephan Thernstrom, *Poverty and Progress: Social Mobility in a Nineteenth-Century City* (Cambridge: Harvard University, 1964), pp. 34, 42.

10. Marvin Meyers, *The Jacksonian Persuasion* (New York: Random House, Vintage, 1960); David Rothman, *The Discovery of the Asylum* (Boston: Little, Brown, 1971); Michael B. Katz, *The Irony of Early School Reform: Educational Innovation in Mid-Nineteenth Century Massachusetts* (Cambridge: Harvard University, 1968).

11. Quoted phrases from David Donald, "An Excess of Democracy: The American Civil War and the Social Process," in his *Lincoln Reconsidered,* 2d ed. (New York: Random House Vintage, 1960), pp. 223, 229. See also Stanley Elkins, *Slavery: A Problem in American Institutional and Intellectual Life* (New York: Grosset & Dunlap, Universal Library, 1963), pt. IV.

ety characterized by functional specialization and impersonality. Reform movements during the later nineteenth and early twentieth centuries, according to Wiebe, were reactions to and reflections of this change.[12]

Sociologists of community have dated the breakdown in yet more recent times. Roland Warren and Maurice Stein, the most notable and most historically conscious of these sociologists, are somewhat imprecise, but they seem inclined to place the beginnings of what Warren calls the "great change" in the 1920s.[13] With Stein and Warren, the sociological idea we have been pursuing through American historiography returns to the sociologists.

It would be gravely misleading—and unfair—to ignore the uniqueness of each of the historical interpretations I have been discussing. Each scholar has phrased his crucial transformation in an individual fashion, and each has made an important contribution to our understanding of the past. But there is an underlying and troublesome logic common to all of them. Each treats the change as *the* great change in which the scales were decisively tipped in favor of modernity, and the notion is based upon the same unidirectional and unilinear logic considered in the previous chapter.

The absorption of this logic into historical thinking at a time when the professional organization of historical scholarship encourages concentration on rather short historical periods within which, not between or among which, most research is undertaken has produced some rather curious results. If these books are placed in serial order, they offer a picture of community breakdown repeating itself in the 1650s, 1690s, 1740s, 1780s, 1820s, 1850s, 1880s, and 1920s. Each captures important dimensions of social change, but their dependence upon the community breakdown thesis limits their value for anyone concerned with the processes and consequences of social change over an extended period. While it is essential for me to acknowledge the contribution of these works to American historiog-

12. Robert H. Wiebe, *The Search for Order, 1877–1920* (New York: Hill & Wang, 1967), pp. xiii–xiv.
13. Roland Warren, *The Community in America* (Chicago: Rand McNally, 1963); Maurice Stein, *The Eclipse of Community* (New York: Harper, 1964).

raphy and to my own understanding of the past, it is also necessary to say that collectively they do not advance our understanding as much as they seem to when singly approached. General references to community breakdown fail these books when they are considered together and when our interest is in a longer expanse of American history than the customs of the historical profession usually offer.

The framework of "decay and dissolution," as James Henretta has recently called it, is most evident in the recent historiography of the colonial period.[14] The ancestry of this approach to colonial history is difficult to trace. Henretta suggests that the interpretation may go back as far as Frederick Jackson Turner. Although he is probably correct in a very general sense, I suspect that a more direct line can be drawn to the work of Perry Miller. Although Miller was greatly interested in the work of Turner, he apparently got the idea of decay from the Puritan sources he knew so well, and he called it, quite properly in the context of Puritanism, "declension." Later, however, other scholars converted this idea, initially grounded in the historical record, into sociological language, in which the vocabulary of decline was pervasive, especially in the 1940s when the translation seems to have occurred.[15]

The logic of social theory thus entered colonial historiography largely unnoticed, which made it harder for historians to detect its influence on their work. Two scholars who have made enormous contributions to historical writing by using the social sciences to expand the subject matter and methodology of historical scholarship, Oscar Handlin and Bernard Bailyn, seem to have played a central role in transforming Miller's theological idea, rooted in history, into a sociological one with a tendency to escape from history. Much of the work cited above has come from their seminars at

14. James Henretta, "The Morphology of New England Society in the Colonial Period," *JIH*, 2 (1971): 380. See also Zuckerman, "Fabrication of Identity in Early America."
15. Miller, "Declension in a Bible Commonwealth." On the notion of decline in American social science during this period, see C. Wright Mills, "The Professional Ideology of the Social Pathologists," in his *Power, Politics and People*, ed. Irving L. Horowitz (New York: Oxford University Press, 1963), pp. 525–552.

Harvard University.[16] Although the crucial distinction between historical data and sociological idea is often, though not always, evident in their own work, monographic studies building upon their work, whether by their own students or by others in the profession, typically assume that the sociological idea is a historical fact.

◆

Neither the logic of decay, nor, for that matter, a logic of uniform growth can open up new questions in the way Redfield did in his response to Lewis. They seem, in fact, to narrow the range of relevant evidence and reduce the number of questions that might be asked of community in American history. What is needed is an alternative to this restrictive logic, an approach that can respond in a more open manner to the concrete complexity of structural change in the American past.

Consideration of another group of historical works may help clarify the directions in which we can and should move. The studies just examined implicitly drew upon the community decline thesis for their narrative form. Now I want to turn to several recent works that take social change and community as their explicit subject. Rowland Berthoff and Robert Wiebe have attempted to explain the principle of American social organization in studies that cover the

16. Handlin learned his social theory while participating in an interdisciplinary project in Harvard's Department of Social Relations, a department at that time largely associated with Parsons. Bailyn, who studied under both Handlin and Miller, had, in addition, close personal and intellectual associations with the theorists at Columbia's Bureau of Applied Social Research. Paul Lazarsfeld was one of the major figures at Columbia, and Bailyn married his daughter Lotte and, with her, coauthored *Massachusetts Shipping, 1697–1714* (Cambridge: Harvard University, 1959), a book that relied heavily upon social science methodology. Although his work on the merchants was not shaped by social theory (though it was influenced by it), the book on education published in 1960 was. Columbia's sociologists influenced history in another way. The history department at Columbia, especially Richard Hofstadter, established close relations with the sociologists. All but two of the historians discussed above either were trained at Harvard, usually under Handlin or Bailyn, or were associated with Columbia as teachers or students in the 1950s: Handlin, Bailyn, Bushman, Wood, Rothman, Lane, Thernstrom, Katz at Harvard; Donald, Meyers, Elkins at Columbia.

whole sweep of American history.[17] It is impossible to summarize their full arguments here, especially Wiebe's richly complex evocation of the changing "units of life" in American history. The two books, moreover, are radically different in ideological orientation and in intellectual style, yet they share an instructive common approach to the problem of social change and community. Berthoff's *Unsettled People* and Wiebe's *Segmented Society* both begin with the tightly knit organic communities of the colonial period, and each shows the evolution of a modern American society in which the fundamental units of social cohesion are large-scale organizations and status orientations that are identified with the national economic and occupational structure.

Yet the pattern of stages unfolding between the colonial period and our own time differs in these two books. In Berthoff's vision, the communal society of the colonial era collapsed in the nineteenth century, producing an atomized and chaotic social experience for Americans. In the twentieth century, however, there emerged a new principle of social integration based upon the presence of large-scale organizations, mostly corporate businesses. Berthoff sees in this development the promise of a stability lost since the colonial period. Wiebe, who does not share Berthoff's conservative ideology, is less optimistic about the present and more inclined to see a satisfactory level of order in the nineteenth century. He argues that the tight communal pattern of the colonial period was replaced in the nineteenth century by locality-based units of society. This nineteenth-century pattern has in turn been replaced in the twentieth century by functional segments associated largely with the economic realm. Wiebe sees three successive and distinct patterns of social integration: the first communal, the second locality based, and the third made up of bureaucratic segments. Berthoff's model, by contrast, is one of integration, disintegration, and reintegration. Although in Berthoff's scheme, order has been restored in the mid-twentieth cen-

17. Rowland Berthoff, *An Unsettled People: Social Order and Disorder in American History* (New York: Harper, 1971); Robert H. Wiebe, *The Segmented Society* (New York: Oxford University Press, 1975).

tury, the communal ties that were central to colonial society seem to be lost forever. In both of these studies, they belong to an earlier stage of development.[18]

Each of these studies might be criticized for its failure to explain with some precision the process whereby one stage passes into the next, but there is another, more important, conceptual failure that characterizes them both. By defining in temporal terms the tension between community and other forms of social cohesion (or in Berthoff's case, the alleged lack of cohesion), neither book can deal adequately with the ongoing tension between communal and noncommunal experiences in the daily lives of men and women throughout our history.[19]

Another version of this notion of the sequential relationship between community and modern patterns of association can be found in Michael H. Frisch's book, *Town into City: Springfield, Massachusetts, and the Meaning of Community, 1840-1880*. Perhaps the most thoughtful study we have of the changing structure and meaning of community in America, it shares the same conceptual flaw that I have traced in the sociological literature and now in much of the historical literature. Beginning his study in 1840, Frisch acknowledges an "emerging social diversity" in Springfield over a long period of time, but he insists that in all essential respects the town's "traditional culture still retained great power, and people still lived among the institutions and ideas it had nurtured." There was still a local sense of community that was reminiscent of life one hundred years before. Residents of the community, he indicates, "tended to think, act, and view their community in direct, personal, informal, and nonabstract terms." The next few decades, however, saw a fundamental transformation in the definition of community. By the 1880s, men and women experienced a "substitution of formality for informality." The experiential community was re-

18. But note Wiebe's undeveloped remark on this point in ibid., p. 25.

19. Bernard W. Sheehan makes this point in a review of Berthoff's book in the *WMQ*, 30 (1973): 154–157. This flaw is more serious in Berthoff's book, but it is also apparent in Wiebe's.

placed by a new kind of social identification that was far more abstract.[20]

Phrased in the terms I have been using, Frisch argues that the social organization of American life, even on the local level, shifted from gemeinschaft to gesellschaft. Hence, he offers sequences virtually identical to those found in conventional social theory. Again, there is no discussion of the interplay of communal and noncommunal experiences or of conflict between different groups within the city that may vary in the degrees of their orientation to gemeinschaft or gesellschaft dimensions of social life.

This latter possibility, that some identifiable social groups are more community or locality oriented than others, has entered historiography under the rubric of Robert Merton's local–cosmopolitan terminology. Several historians have used this distinction to classify political groupings in the era of the American Revolution.[21] The adaptation of Merton's notion one finds in the work of Samuel P. Hays, however, provides a more useful comparison with Frisch's approach. In a series of notable articles, Hays stresses the same structural changes accompanying urbanization that one finds in Frisch's account: the processes of centralization, bureaucratization, and role segmentation and the development of an abstract notion of community. Yet Hays also notes the persistence of more local and personal units of social cohesion based upon networks of kin, friendship, and ethnic solidarity. Both patterns, Hays argues, existed in the city, though he tends to identify each of these forms of social cohesion with distinct social classes.[22] Hays makes an important

20. Michael H. Frisch, *Town into City: Springfield, Massachusetts, and the Meaning of Community, 1840–1880* (Cambridge: Harvard University, 1972), pp. 33, 48, 49, 246–247.

21. For Merton's formulation, see his *Social Theory and Social Structure*, rev. ed. (New York: Free Press, 1957), pp. 387–420. For the uses by historians, see, for example, Jackson Turner Main, *Political Parties before the Constitution* (Chapel Hill: University of North Carolina, 1973); James Kirby Martin, *Men in Rebellion* (New Brunswick, N.J.: Rutgers, 1973); Van Beck Ball, *Politics without Parties: Massachusetts, 1780–1791* (Pittsburgh: University of Pittsburgh, 1972); and Stephen E. Patterson, *Political Parties in Revolutionary Massachusetts* (Madison: University of Wisconsin, 1973).

22. Samuel P. Hays, "A Systematic Social History," in *American History*, ed. George A. Billias and Gerald N. Grob (New York: Free Press, 1971), pp. 315–366; idem., "Political Parties and the Community–Society Continuum," in *The American*

theoretical contribution by allowing for the persistence of traditional and communal patterns of social interaction even under
modern industrial conditions. This work, along with Herbert
Gutman's studies of the American working class, reveals that traditional values and patterns of behavior do not passively collapse before larger processes of social change.[23]

Hays does fall short, though, of an even more important theoretical
breakthrough. By associating gemeinschaft with one class and
gesellschaft with another, he misses the importance to the lives of
the whole population of the interplay of these two patterns of social
cohesion in modern society. The working classes, labeled "locals" by
Hays, are involved in large-scale organizations, from their places of
work to the educational bureaucracy that takes care of their children's education. Conversely, members of the upper class have
families, friends, and other communal forms of social relations.[24]
Where they perhaps differ is in the relative importance of the two
dimensions of their lives in particular contexts, especially in politics.
There may also be differences in the way they reconcile whatever
dissonance is produced by living in both worlds, gemeinschaft and
gesellschaft. If so, however, this is a historical question to be
empirically investigated, not something to be assumed.

If we are to get at the full complexity of the communal experience
in American history, it is essential to avoid both the simple sequential model whereby gesellschaft replaces gemeinschaft and the

Party Systems: Stages of Political Development, ed. William N. Chambers and Walter
D. Burnham (New York: Oxford University Press, 1967), pp. 152–181; idem., "The
Politics of Reform in Municipal Government in the Progressive Era," *Pacific Northwest Quarterly,* 55 (1964): 157–169; and idem., "The Changing Political Structure
of the City in Industrial America," *JUH,* 1 (1974): 6–38.

23. See Herbert G. Gutman, *Work, Culture and Society in Industrializing America*
(New York: Knopf, 1976), and idem., *The Black Family in Slavery and Freedom,
1750–1925* (New York: Pantheon, 1976).

24. There is also a sort of implied derogation of locals, something that seems to
have been associated with the local–cosmopolitan notion from its inception. Hays, in
his most recent work, occasionally suggests that he believes that the upper classes
may be involved in both centralized and localized social units. The lives of the less-
well-off classes, however, remain, in his view, bounded by the parochial and localistic
outlook. See his "The Development of Pittsburgh as a Social Order," *Western Pennsylvania History Magazine,* 57 (1974): 431–148.

model that associates gemeinschaft with one social group and
gesellschaft with another. These two dimensions of social experience transcend social groupings.

◆

A more useful narrative structure for considering the changing
place of community in American history can be built upon these
sociological and historical foundations. It will have to acknowledge
that it is possible to speak broadly of a sequence of different forms
for the dominant units of life in American history, but it will also
have to recognize the extent to which this process has been cumula-
tive and has affected all social classes. As new patterns overlay the
old, the older communal units of social cohesion persist. The task of
the historian is not to write their obituary, but rather to discover
their changing role in people's lives.

A recent essay by John Higham is suggestive of a new framework.
Although he stresses (more than I would) the "sequential unfolding
of three forms of unity" in American history, he tentatively, if a bit
ambiguously, observes that earlier forms live on in their successors.
His undeveloped point that Americans "have commonly been
enmeshed in divergent systems of integration" might provide an
appropriate starting point for the theoretical and empirical work of
historians of community.[25]

This endeavor implies a perspective that comprehends the simultaneous polarity and reciprocity of gemeinschaft and gesellschaft as
patterns of human interaction. By viewing communal and noncommunal ways as two elements in a bifurcated society, the historian has an adequate framework for observing the changing structure and meaning of community over time. Because it assumes the
coexistence of communal and noncommunal ways, the notion of a

25. John Higham, "Hanging Together: Divergent Unities in American History,"
JAH, 61 (1974): 7. After completing his discussion of adhesive forces in the sequential manner I have here criticized, Higham remarks that "a deeper examination
of historical experience" would probably reveal the interplay of these unities. Each,
he observes, "has something to contribute to our complex society, and each of them
survives within it" (ibid., p. 28).

bifurcated society allows historians to recognize the change without becoming trapped by the logic of sequence that is part of the inevitable social-thesis approach to community. Freed of this ahistorical logic, the cultural historian and critic can become engaged in a disciplined and empirical analysis of the ways in which the roles, statuses, and identities held by individual Americans changed over time.

Community cannot be studied in isolation. If one is studying community in a complex society, one must consider it in the context of larger social aggregates and in comparison with other forms of solidarity within a given society. Study of a single locality or social segment will not, as Eric Wolf points out, illuminate the dynamics of a complex society.[26] Perhaps the image of a social field in which there are various kinds of social groupings, one of which is communal, provides the necessary breadth of view.[27] Such a metaphor ought to direct the historian's attention to the "multiple loyalties" that, as David Potter has observed, are a basic fact of social life in complex societies.[28] Some of these loyalties are to communities, while others may be related to one's position in a larger and more abstract category, for example, *professional, corporate employee, homeowner, citizen.*

From this perspective, the historian will ask how people manage to live, simultaneously, in radically different social worlds: one communal, and the others associational, or perhaps even entirely abstract. How do men and women define the boundaries between these various social groupings? How do they define their loyalties and take and develop roles? Which of the orientations, communal or noncommunal, is most salient in shaping their actions? Which social role or pattern of social relations is dominant under what specific

26. Eric R. Wolf, "Aspects of Group Relations in a Complex Society: Mexico," *AA,* 58 (1956): esp. pp. 1066, 1074.

27. Börge Hanssen, "Fields of Social Activity and Their Dynamics," *Translations of the Westermarck Society,* 2 (1953): 99–133. For the original formulation of this metaphor, see Kurt Lewin, *Field Theory in Social Science,* ed. D. Cartwright (New York: Harper, 1951).

28. David Potter, *History and American Society,* ed. Don E. Fehrenbacher (New York: Oxford University Press, 1973), p. 55.

conditions or circumstances? How has the relationship between these two orientations changed over time? How does it differ among identifiable social groups? How do the connections between them— the adaptive mechanisms devised for bridging them—change over time? How do the two patterns interrelate and influence each other? When do they reenforce each other? What happens when they provide, in Max Weber's language, "contradictory systems of order?"[29] How is the resulting psychological dissonance resolved in terms of social action?[30]

The social experience of seventeenth-century Americans, with the possible exception of a few members of the elite, was not divided between communal and noncommunal ways. The "whole of life" was framed by a "circle of loved, familiar faces, known and fondled objects."[31] Men and women did not have the compartmentalized lives that characterize modern society; one set of standards circumscribed them as whole men and women. The process of social change over the next two centuries altered all of this. I am referring here to societal change, that is, change in the social system itself, not simply alterations within the system.[32] The structure and meaning of community was transformed in the process, but it was not eclipsed. Communal and noncommunal ways were gradually distinguished from each other, and the distinctions between public and private spheres of life were sharpened. The mass of Americans became involved in two distinct but intertwined patterns of social relations, one communal, the other not. The experience of community that developed is best understood as one dimension of life in a bifurcated society, and this phenomenon is what Tönnies originally sought to explain.

29. Max Weber, *The Theory of Social and Economic Organization*, trans. Talcott Parsons (New York: Free Press, 1964), p. 125.
30. For an important discussion of these psychological issues, see Leon Festinger, *A Theory of Cognitive Dissonance* (Stanford: Stanford University, 1957).
31. Peter Laslett, *The World We Have Lost*, 2d. ed. (New York: Scribner's, 1971), p. 21. He refers to England about 1600, but this statement applies equally well to seventeenth-century British America.
32. On the distinction, see Wilbert E. Moore, *Social Change* (Englewood Cliffs, N.J.: Prentice-Hall, 1963), pp. 5–6, and A. R. Radcliffe-Brown, *A Natural Science of Society* (New York: Free Press, 1957), p. 87.

If the seventeenth century was characterized by a convergence of roles, modern society multiplies and separates social roles. Whatever one thinks of Herbert Spencer's social philosophy in general, surely he was correct when he settled upon differentiation as the fundamental process that defined modernization. Modern urban society is a social aggregate in which different activities, ranging from worship and play to work and politics, each generate or occur within different networks of social interaction.[33] Each of these also provides a reference group that forms a portion of modern man's identity. Perhaps each of these networks has its own special quality as a form of social interaction that deserves special classification. As my purposes are, however, to explore only community, social phenomena can be divided into two classes: communal and noncommunal. By thus isolating community, it is possible to trace its changing meanings within the context of the larger structural changes that occurred during three centuries of American history.

Locality as Community, 1630–1870

In his classic study of the English villager in the thirteenth century, George C. Homans offered a wonderfully simple criterion of the integrity of local life: "The men of the village had upon the whole more contacts with one another than they had with outsiders."[34] The same can be said of the men and women who lived in seventeenth-century American villages and towns. In fact, as we shall see, this statement is descriptive of the social experience of most Americans until the middle of the nineteenth century. In modern America, however, locality, with very few exceptions, no longer has this social significance. What follows is an attempt to determine the changing significance of locality as community in the seventeenth, eighteenth, and nineteenth centuries.

By casting a historian's eye over such a long period of social

33. Charles Tilly, *An Urban World* (Boston: Little, Brown, 1974), p. 28.
34. George C. Homans, *English Villagers of the Thirteenth Century* (Cambridge: Harvard University, 1941), p. 403.

change, it is possible to isolate fundamental from more superficial alterations in the character of community. There is a great deal of continuity. For much of this long period, the experience of community was found through the personal contacts that marked the daily rounds of local life. Community as a place and community as an experience were one. Some time before our own era, however, this linkage was shattered. One of my purposes is to understand the timing and process of this change, yet I do not want to overemphasize this intention because it would direct attention away from the continual changes in the configuration, intensity, and meaning of community that occurred even during those decades when locality clearly remained the basis of community. The task before us is to explore the diversity and constant change within various historical patterns of community. Our present knowledge on these issues is not extensive, but I have taken the materials available and proceeded to frame a tentative and speculative conceptual framework that can provide a starting point for building a detailed empirical account of American communities.

The Colonial Period

At the beginning of the seventeenth century, when England sent her first colonists to the New World, most Englishmen (perhaps 80 percent) lived in an intensely local and predominately oral culture.[35] There was little institutional centralization in the body politic, no royal bureaucracy. Hence, each of several hundred provincial communities was "consciously separate" and often "surprisingly different."[36] All of this nourished localism as a cultural value.

It was just during this period, however, that these pervasive local values were being challenged by innovations in the economic and political realms. The first impulses of economic modernization threatened the traditional role of the "local community as a unit of

35. Lawrence Cremin, *American Education: The Colonial Experience* (New York: Harper, 1970), p. 227.
36. Alan Everitt, *Change in the Provinces: The Seventeenth Century* (Leicester, England: University of Leicester, 1969), p. 6.

employment or of social security."[37] This crisis in village life produced misery and suffering—and levels of geographical mobility that have surprised historians who had assumed a static village life.[38] Local loyalties remained strong, nonetheless, and few migrated far. Nine out of ten Englishmen, it appears, died within ten miles of their places of birth.[39] The general commitment to localism in Stuart England is also apparent in resistance to Charles I's attempt to exert authority over local English institutions. Resistance to Stuart centralization and sensitivity to the ways in which economic modernization was threatening traditional patterns of community may have heightened the commitment to localism in the very culture that would soon supply settlers for North America.[40]

Those who migrated to the New World, particularly those who came as part of the great Puritan migration, carried this commitment to community with them. John Winthrop, their leader, expressed their communal ideal in a lay sermon he delivered on board the *Arbella* before the main contingent of Puritans landed in Massachusetts Bay in 1630:

> We must entertain each other in brotherly affection, we must be willing to abridge ourselves of our superfluities, for the supply of others' necessities; we must uphold a familiar commerce together, . . . in all meekness, patience and liberality. We must delight in each other, make others' conditions our own, rejoice together, mourn together, labor and suffer together.[41]

The Puritans were remarkably successful in making local life communal in the villages they established. With astonishing rapidity,

37. Christopher Hill, *Society and Puritanism in Pre-Revolutionary England*, 2d. ed. (New York: Schocken, 1967), p. 483.
38. For the crucial study in this "discovery" of mobility, see Peter Laslett and John Harrison, "Clayworth and Cogenhoe," in *Historical Essays, 1600–1750: Presented to David Ogg* (New York: Barnes & Noble, 1963), pp. 157–184.
39. Robert L. Goodman, "Newbury, Massachusetts, 1635–1685: The Social Foundations of Harmony and Conflict" (Ph.D. diss., Michigan State University, 1974), p. 27.
40. T. H. Breen, "Persistent Localism: English Social Change and the Shaping of New England Institutions," *WMQ*, 32 (1975): 3–28.
41. John Winthrop, "A Model of Christian Charity," in *The Puritens*, ed. Perry Miller and Thomas Johnson, 2 vols. (New York: Harper, 1963), vol. I, p. 198.

these villages achieved a communal life "more deeply rooted, more permanent" than what had been left in England.[42]

These communities were built upon primordial feelings and drew upon custom, but they were socially constructed and not the precipitate of tradition.[43] This circumstance makes these communities, reactionary in so many respects, profoundly modern. Based upon a written covenant, these communities were the product of decision rather than peasant inertia. Christopher Hill has extended this logic one step farther. Making reference to the English situation, he has called the communal forms devised by the Puritans "contract communities" (in contradistinction to "status communities"). But such a formulation would be misleading for New England.[44] It suggests a limited Lockean compact or even a nineteenth-century American business contract (always strictly construed), when in fact the covenant created broad obligations based upon a fusion of reason and emotion. Although the towns of New England were established by signing a covenant and newcomers were admitted in the same way, membership was fundamentally spiritual and experiential, often based upon previous and long-established friendship.[45]

The process of community building was not easy. Signing the covenant did not create a mystical bond among the men and women settling in a single locality. Although the existence of family or premigration acquaintances made integration into the community easier, many settlers, perhaps half, moved on to two or three settle-

42. John Murrin, "Review Essay," *HT*, 11 (1972): 231. See also Philip J. Greven, Jr., *Four Generations: Population, Land and Family in Colonial Andover, Massachusetts* (Ithaca, N.Y.: Cornell University, 1970), pp. 268–269, and John J. Waters, "Hingham, Massachusetts, 1631–1661: An East Anglian Oligarchy in the New World," *JSH*, 1 (1967–1968): 370. Cf. W. R. Prest, "Stability and Change in Old and New England: Clayworth and Dedham," *JIH*, 6 (1976): 359–374.

43. For a perceptive discussion of this concept, see Gerald D. Suttles, *The Social Construction of Communities* (Chicago: University of Chicago, 1972).

44. Hill, *Society and Puritanism*, p. 491.

45. On the nature of the covenant, see Kenneth Lockridge, *A New England Town: The First Hundred Years* (New York: Norton, 1970), chap. 1; Goodman, "Newbury," chaps. 1–2. Daniel Calhoun, *Professional Lives in America: Structure and Aspiration, 1750–1850* (Cambridge: Harvard University, 1965), p. 132. Page Smith points out that the formation of covenanted communities remained significant well into the nineteenth century. See his *As a City upon a Hill: The Town in American History* (Cambridge: Massachusetts Institute of Technology, 1973).

ments in quick succession until they found a village made up of like-minded men and women.[46] This process of sorting out was facilitated by the diversity of towns, which differed, sometimes substantially, in institutional forms and cultural styles. Such pluralism, the product of the intense commitment to localism in respect to church and state that the Puritans carried across the Atlantic, thus nourished communal solidarity in New England. There were, of course, limits to this local autonomy, and the General Court did intervene in the affairs of deviant communities, but the Puritans generally relied upon a shared ideology rather than upon centralized institutional power to ensure societal uniformity and cohesion.[47]

Although Kenneth Lockridge exaggerates when he writes that the New England town was a "self-contained social unit, almost hermetically sealed off from the rest of the world," his point is well taken.[48] The local community had a closed quality that is evident even in the physical layout. Whether built upon the ribbon or the cluster pattern, the town plan and the manner in which land was distributed suggests limited expectations for growth, surely nothing of the spirit one finds in town promotions in the middle and late nineteenth century.[49]

The local community provided within itself a focus for the economic, political, social, and religious lives of the townspeople. It was not so much a segment of the larger commonwealth as it was a miniature of the commonwealth. If the town did not form a "whole" society for the people who lived there, writes Linda Bissell, "it contained the most important human contacts."[50] There was infrequent resort to outside institutions, and the norm was for endogamous

46. Linda A. Bissell, "From One Generation to Another: Mobility in Seventeenth-Century Windsor, Connecticut," *WMQ*, 31 (1974): 81, 95; John J. Waters, *The Otis Family in Provincial and Revolutionary Massachusetts* (Chapel Hill: University of North Carolina, 1968), chap. 1; Goodman, "Newbury," pp. 38–40.

47. George L. Haskins, *Law and Authority in Early Massachusetts* (New York: Macmillan, 1960), pp. 69, 84; John Higham, "Hanging Together," p. 11.

48. Lockridge, *A New England Town*, p. 64.

49. See David J. Russo, *Families and Communities* (Nashville: American Association for State and Local History, 1974), p. 27. For a good sample of town plans, see John Reps, *The Making of Urban America* (Princeton: Princeton University, 1965).

50. Linda A. Bissell, "Family, Friends, and Neighbors: Social Interaction in Seventeenth Century Windsor, Connecticut" (Ph.D. diss., Brandeis, 1973), p. 8.

marriages, though small numbers sometimes made this impossible.[51] The tight pattern of informal and intimate social interaction was, for all intents, organically complete.

The economic life of New England drew men to the town as effectively as did the religious and social ideals they shared. There was no conflict between the ideology of community and the structure of the economy. The land grants of the General Court were made only to towns or to groups committed to establishing towns. The town, therefore, was the institution that made land available to individuals. In fact, the town did more than this. Records of town meetings reveal that the town also managed the local economy. It built roads, arranged land-use patterns, ordered fencing, and the like. Even the debt network seems to have been localized, and gifts, as measured by bequests in wills, seldom went to persons or charities outside of the testator's home village.[52]

One must not, however, imagine a situation of complete economic isolation. Even the smallest village had some trade beyond its immediate neighborhood. Dedham traded with Boston, and Andover sold produce to Salem in exchange for cloth, paper, tobacco, salt, pins, powder, nails, knives, and other items. Windsor, Connecticut, was sufficiently involved in translocal trade to feel the effects of worldwide depressions. Yet the economy was fundamentally local, and trading relationships were generally familial and intimate.[53]

Townsmen did trade, but their lives were not shaped or even touched by participation in an abstract and competitive market society; they were in the market, but not of it. Like people living in

51. Susan L. Norton, "Marital Migration in Essex County, Massachusetts, in the Colonial and Early Federal Periods," *Journal of Marriage and the Family*, 35 (1973): 406–418.

52. Bushman, *From Puritan to Yankee*, chap. 1; Lockridge, *A New England Town;* Haskins, *Law and Authority*, p. 70. On debts, see Jessica K. Ehrlich, "A Town Study in Colonial New York: New Town, Queens County (1642–1790)" (Ph.D. diss., Michigan, 1974), p. 154, which considered a Long Island town; on gifts, see Kenneth Lockridge, *Literacy in Colonial New England* (New York: Norton, 1974), p. 34.

53. J. Franklin Jameson, ed., *Johnson's Wonder Working Providence* (New York: Scribner's, 1910), p. 179; Greven, *Four Generations*, p. 68; Bissell, "Family, Friends, and Neighbors," pp. 26, 33; and Smith *As a City upon a Hill*, pp. 86–87.

many peasant societies today, these New Englanders were involved in trade, but these economic activities were deeply embedded in an organic pattern of life. Trade did not dominate local society; rather, it was itself dominated by local society. Of course, there were occasional examples of urban and commercial activity outside of this context even in the seventeenth century, but the intrusion of these ways into the overwhelming majority of local communities would almost certainly have meant a social and moral crisis.[54]

The town, not the individual, was the basic unit of political representation.[55] Political decisions were made through "discussion" and consensus rather than through interest-group conflict. Votes were seldom recorded in the minutes of town meetings. When decisions were made, the town records indicate simply that they were reached "by general agreement."[56] Even on matters larger than itself, the town characteristically expressed itself as a unit.

Religious life was similarly bounded by the town. Within the confines of a colony-wide consensus on ideology, each local congregation went its own way. The strength of this localism was apparent in the controversy over the Halfway Covenant. After the consociation of ministers agreed on the doctrine, many found themselves unable to persuade their own towns and congregations to vote for and implement the policy.[57]

The family and the Christian fellowship provided the basis for local life. Family, church, and town provided overlapping contexts of life. One's social roles as father, neighbor, fellow Christian,

54. See the account of the fragmentation of Salem in Paul Boyer and Stephen Nissenbaum, *Salem Possessed: The Social Origins of Witchcraft* (Cambridge: Harvard University, 1974).

55. See Oscar Handlin and Mary Handlin, eds., *The Popular Sources of Political Authority* (Cambridge: Harvard University, 1966); J. R. Pole, *Political Representation in England and the Origins of the American Republic* (New York: St. Martin's, 1966).

56. Lockridge, *A New England Town*, p. 54. For more on this consensual local politics, see Michael Zuckerman, "The Social Context of Democracy in Massachusetts," *WMQ*, 25 (1968): 523–544; idem., *Peaceable Kingdoms: New England Towns in the Eighteenth Century* (New York: Knopf, 1970).

57. Dedham provides such an example. See Lockridge, *A New England Town*, p. 34. See also Robert G. Pope, *The Half-Way Covenant* (Princeton: Princeton University, 1969).

farmer, town official, all converged. The town was essentially homogeneous: It had one religious belief, a unified political vision, even a fairly even distribution of wealth and a narrow range of occupations. It was a remarkably undifferentiated society, and it was difficult to draw the line between family and community, private and public.[58]

To what extent can these generalizations, based upon studies of New England, be extended to the middle and southern colonies? Local, homogeneous units of life were nearly as pervasive there, though they took different forms. The traditional contrast between homogeneous New England and the heterogeneous middle colonies, is, I think, both true and misleading. While more homogeneous than New York, Massachusetts was not without diversity from the colony-wide perspective. Although there was greater ethnic and religious homogeneity in Massachusetts, the cultures of the individual communities still differed in ways that were real to the men and women who lived in them and—perhaps more pointedly—to those who moved on.[59] Like-minded people sorted themselves out among the diverse Massachusetts towns; the same thing occurred, in more obvious ways, in the middle colonies, where the differences among towns were sharper. Men and women sharing particular cultural values came together to form the small, intensely parochial, local units of life that made up the kaleidoscopic American social landscape.[60]

American society, as a whole, approximated an open society. The 260 churches of the British colonies at the end of the seventeenth

58. Oscar Handlin and Mary Handlin, *The Dimensions of Liberty* (New York: Atheneum, 1966), pp. 68, 114–115; Boyer and Nissenbaum, *Salem Possessed*, p. 151. David H. Flaherty's *Privacy in Colonial New England* (Charlottesville: University of Virginia, 1972) argues for a great deal of privacy, but he supplies massive evidence demonstrating its extraordinarily limited nature by any modern standard.

59. There was even some important ethnic diversity in New England. See David T. Konig, "A New Look at the Essex 'French': Ethnic Frictions and Community Tensions in Seventeenth Century Essex County, Massachusetts," *Essex Institute Historical Collections*, 110 (1974): 167–180.

60. G. B. Warden, "L'urbanisation Américaine avant 1800," *Annales*, 25 (1970): 867; Patricia U. Bonomi, *A Factious People: Politics and Society in Colonial New York* (New York: Columbia University, 1971), p. 27.

century included 116 Congregational, 71 Anglican, 15 Baptist, 17 Dutch Reformed, 15 Presbyterian, 12 French Reformed, 9 Roman Catholic, and 5 Lutheran, plus small communities of Quakers, Mennonites, Huguenots, Anabaptists, and Jews.[61] These figures, however, must be interpreted with care; they do not mean that the colonists daily experienced religious and cultural diversity. These data refer to the whole of colonial America, not to the local, homogeneous, and closed enclaves in which men and women lived the near totality of their lives. Colonial America was, then, a heterogeneous culture made up of homogeneous and largely isolated individual units.

The settlement patterns in the middle colonies reveal a strong tendency toward the segregation of cultural groups. Benjamin Franklin pointed this out in his famous complaint of 1755 that the "Palatine Boors" of Pennsylvania "by herding together establish their language and Manners to the Exclusion of ours."[62] The Germans were not the only such group; the Pennsylvania landscape, according to the geographer James Lemon, was dotted with settlements of Welsh, Scotch-Irish, Quakers, and Mennonites as well.[63]

Tightly knit communities were also common in New York. The Dutch in New Netherlands, in fact, had explicitly urged settlers to imitate the New England fashion of settling into villages. Later, under English rule, communities often were established on the basis of patents that served much the same purpose as a covenant in New

61. Cremin, *American Education*, pp. 163–164.

62. Benjamin Franklin, "Observations Concerning the Increase of Mankind," in *The Papers of Benjamin Franklin*, ed. Leonard W. Labaree, 13 vols. to date (New Haven: Yale University, 1959–), 4:234. For New York, see Bonomi, *A Factious People*, pp. 25–29, 54–55; idem., "Local Government in Colonial New York: A Base for Republicanism," in *Aspects of Early New York Society and Politics*, ed. Jacob Judd and Irwin Polishook (Tarrytown, N.Y.: Sleepy Hollow Restorations, 1974), pp. 44, 49–50.

63. James Lemon, *The Best Poor Man's Country: A Geographical Study of Early Southeastern Pennsylvania* (Baltimore: Johns Hopkins, 1972), pp. 43–45, 99–103, 109–110. Lemon does not present his data in a manner that allows an assessment of how exclusive these settlements might have been, but it appears that there were fairly tight cultural units in spite of the prevailing "open-country" pattern of settlement. See also Lester J. Cappon, ed., *Atlas of Early American History* (Princeton: Princeton University, 1976), p. 24.

England, and new persons were admitted into the town only with the consent of the "whole towns inhabitants."[64] In a tract written to promote settlement in New York, Daniel Denton explained in 1670 that the "usual way" of settling a town was for a group to select a site and petition the governor for a "Grant or Patent" enabling them to form a town. With this authority in hand, he went on, the group can proceed "to settle the place, and take in what inhabitants to themselves they shall see cause to admit of, till their town be full."[65]

The pattern of subcultural particularism that emerged in New York found expression in the colony's political culture. Political orientations were intensely local and parochial. Throughout the eighteenth century, New York's political life was marked, in Patricia Bonomi's words, by a "jealous attachment to local prerogatives." Economic life was also local in its orientation and essentially informal. The local village or neighborhood, integrated by face-to-face and intimate relationships, often based upon kinship networks, was the colony's basic economic unit.[66]

The South is more complicated, but the work of Carl Bridenbaugh and, more recently, Darrett Rutman and Rhys Isaac reveals the importance of locality-based social patterns of community there. The backcountry was comprised of intensely parochial and clannish settlements established by various cultural groups. While it is true that the more developed tidewater region lacked the compact towns or villages characteristic of New England, the county seems to have served as the basic unit of a vigorous community life in the South. Within this context, with the courthouse as the geographical and social core, one finds a clear pattern of intimate social relationships,

64. Glenn T. Trewartha, "Types of Rural Settlement in Colonial America," *Geographical Review*, 36 (1946): 582–583; Ehrlich, "A Town in Colonial New York," pp. 22 (quotation), 94–95.

65. Daniel Denton, *A Brief Relation of New York* (London: Hancock, 1670), p. 16.

66. Bonomi, "Local Government in Colonial New York," p. 50. Cf. Ehrlich, "A Town Study in Colonial New York." New York City was an exception, but even there, ethnic solidarity within the city was strong. See Thomas J. Archdeacon, *New York City, 1664–1710* (Ithaca N.Y.: Cornell University, 1976). In many parts of the colony, even along the commercially oriented Hudson, this pattern continued to exist in 1800. See Carl Nordstrom, *Frontier Elements in a Hudson River Village* (Port Washington, N.Y.: Kennikat, 1973), pp. 38–39, 45, 53.

kinship networks, and the regular routine of rituals that provide symbolic meanings for such localized and basically oral communities.[67] The differences between the New England town and this geographically more extensive local community are important and deserving of further analysis, but my point here is that it is possible to argue that life was lived in local communities, not only in the colonial North, but given some variation, in the colonial South as well.

———◆———

One must be precise in asserting the claims of community. It is all too easy, especially with the impulse to nostalgia that accompanies most considerations of community, to portray the town, even in New England, with an unwarranted stability. It is also tempting to treat these communities as unchanging during the colonial period. The passage of time brought change. The question, however, is whether this change, which included increased geographic mobility, religious diversity, and the formation of distinct neighborhoods within towns, constitutes a diminution, or even a collapse, of community. While acknowledging these changes, it must be said, I think, that men's and women's lives remained overwhelmingly bounded by local and intimate patterns of human interaction. The fabric of community might have been tugged and stretched, but it was not torn.[68] Kinship networks and the local community continued to shape social experience and, because of intermarriage over the years, may have become, in some respects, even tighter.[69]

Without question, mobility increased during the eighteenth century. The primary cause for this migration seems to have been a

67. Carl Bridenbaugh, *Myths and Realities: Societies of the Colonial South* (New York: Atheneum, 1965), pp. 131–132; Darrett B. Rutman, "The Social Web: A Prospectus for the Study of the Early American Community," in *Insights and Parallels,* ed. William L. O'Neill (Minneapolis: Burgess, 1973), pp. 57–123; Rhys Isaac, "Dramatizing the Ideology of the Revolution: Popular Mobilization in Virginia, 1774–1776," *WMQ,* 33 (1976): 357–385.

68. See Zuckerman, *Peaceable Kingdoms,* p. 258.

69. On the way family groups developed in local communities over the years, see Wendell Hubbard Bash, "Factors Influencing Family and Community Organization in a New England Town, 1730–1940: A Study of Southampton, Massachusetts" (Ph.D. diss., Harvard, 1941), esp. p. 270.

population explosion produced by the exceptionally good health en-
joyed by Europeans in the New World. With the growth of population, it became increasingly difficult for individual towns to provide
sufficient land for the third generation.[70] What does this economically motivated migration mean for the sense of community and kin
that was central to the initial ideal and experience of the towns?
First of all, almost all of the migrations were organized along
familial or community lines. The migrants, bound together as kin or
as members of a mother community, sought land where they could
reestablish the tight pattern of community life they had left. Individual migrants typically moved along the family and friendship
networks thus established.[71] Second, eighteenth-century population
movements seldom involved great distances. The most recent student of transiency in eighteenth-century New England concludes
that most mobility was "localized . . . as transients moved from
town to town within discrete local areas. The long migratory move
. . . was rare."[72]

  Families and communities that were divided by the migration of
subgroups remained in contact in spite of primitive eighteenth-
century communications. Often, moreover, families or other
"colonizing" community subgroups remained in contact with their
"mother" community.[73] The important point, however, is that
migration did not represent a rejection of community or family. It
was, in effect, a way of preserving them when they were threatened

  70. Greven, Four Generations, pp. 123, 213n, and chap. 7; Kenneth Lockridge,
"Land, Population, and the Evolution of New England Society, 1630–1790," PP,
no. 39 (1968), pp. 62–80. Interestingly, there was less mobility and higher community solidarity in the Connecticut valley where the initial settlements had larger
reserves of land for future generations. See Bash, "Factors Influencing Family and
Community Organization," p. 45.
  71. Robert A. Gross, The Minutemen and Their World (New York: Hill & Wang,
1976), p. 82. For evidence of the phenomenon of chain migration, recently discovered in our modern urban society, in premodern colonial America, see Greven,
Four Generations, pp. 157–158, 162, 166.
  72. Douglas L. Jones, "The Strolling Poor: Transiency in Eighteenth Century
Massachusetts," JSH, 8 (1975): 39–40.
  73. See Greven, Four Generations, pp. 166, 215, 254–256. For an English example
of the ways in which ties were maintained, with some suggestion of their intensity,
see Alan MacFarlane, The Family Life of Ralph Josselin: A Seventeenth Century
Clergyman (Cambridge: At the University Press, 1970).

by land scarcity in the original town. The form migration took was in itself an expression of community.

Much the same can be said of the divisions of one town into two or more towns that were so common in the eighteenth century. The division of towns, or the process of "hiving off," produced sixty-five percent of all new towns in eighteenth-century Massachusetts,[74] but this did not imply a dilution of the quest for communal perfection. Indeed, the impulse was usually toward a purer and tighter community. The problem of conflict and diversity, then, was resolved, not by giving up community in favor of modern pluralism, but rather by division. The formation of a new community, whether by division or by migration, created two communities that were both more homogeneous and intense than the preceding single community had been.[75] The advent of division was, in other words, in the service of traditional notions of community.

The practice of dividing towns ended in the nineteenth century, but even in the eighteenth century one finds examples of an alternative to division. Some towns remained whole while developing a series of neighborhoods that defined "separate needs of their own" and had their own "sense of separate identity." In Concord, Massachusetts, for example, town politics were conducted in sectional terms, and the town was "redefined as a confederacy of smaller communities." One might detect in this the roots of modern pluralism, yet it is well to recall that it is also reminiscent of the way in which the "quarters" of the city shaped the political life of thirteenth-century Italian communes.[76]

The neighborhood became the focus of men's and women's lives,

74. This figure is taken from Patterson, *Political Parties in Revolutionary Massachusetts*, p. 36.

75. See Smith, *As a City upon a Hill*, pp. 42–43, and Robert A. East, "Puritanism and New England Settlement," *New England Quarterly*, 17 (1944): 257. An example of the tensions that failure to remove conflict by this method might produce in the absence of any notion of a legitimate pluralistic society may be found in the account of the crisis in Salem in Boyer and Nissenbaum, *Salem Possessed*. For a theoretical statement on the process of purification by migration, see John A. Hostetler, *Amish Society* (Baltimore: Johns Hopkins, 1963), p. 314.

76. Gross, *Minutemen and Their World*, p. 15; The best brief account of these communes may be found in Daniel Waley, *The Italian City-Republics* (New York: McGraw-Hill, 1969).

and families became identified with sections of particular towns. In some cases, a neighborhood became a parish with its own church and with special taxing arrangements, and to that extent, it, rather than the town, became the immediate context of people's lives.[77] While these sectional developments within the town must be recognized, it is equally important to remain cognizant of the small size of the town. The men and women in other sections and in other congregations were not strangers. It was not until the 1750s that even in New York City the first clear indicator of urban anonymity appeared: It was only in this decade that the city's craftsmen began to place newspaper ads for their products. A city directory, another indication of urbanization, first appeared in 1786, and annual editions began in 1790. Even in New York City, the full range of one's social life was lived within neighborhoods and social networks held together by personal interaction and mutual friendship.[78] As late as 1790, however, there were only twenty-four places in the United States with a population over twenty-five hundred people, and in a town or village of this size or smaller, even a sectionally divided one, everyone and everyone's business was known by all.[79]

The politics of the town was embedded in the organic pattern of social relations. The informal and personal relationships that maintained the essential unity of the town also produced a strong impulse toward political consensus.[80] Within the town, this produced a substantial degree of unity, if not always harmony. It also allowed

77. See Murrin, "Review Essay," p. 256n.
78. Michael Kammen, *Colonial New York* (New York: Scribner's, 1975), p. 290; Carl F. Kaestle, *The Evolution of an Urban School System: New York City, 1750–1850* (Cambridge: Harvard University, 1973), p. 35. For a similar argument in respect to Philadelphia in the late eighteenth century, see Sam Bass Warner, Jr., *The Private City: Philadelphia in Three Periods of Its Growth* (Philadelphia: University of Pennsylvania, 1968), chap. 1.
79. Some empirical studies suggest that urban anonymity emerges only after the population of a settlement exceeds something near this figure. See Albert Blumenthal, *Small Town Stuff* (Chicago: University of Chicago, 1932), pp. 101–104.
80. See Zuckerman, "Social Context of Democracy in Massachusetts"; idem., *Peaceable Kingdoms,* but see also the highly critical review by Murrin, "Review Essay." Both Zuckerman and Murrin seem to equate community with harmony. They are distinct notions. On the maintenance of social integration in spite of important institutional change, see Bruce C. Daniels, "Connecticut's Villages Become Mature Towns: The Complexity of Local Institutions, 1676–1776," *WMQ*, 34 (1977): 83–103.

the town to speak to the larger society with one political voice. The votes of Massachusetts towns on matters of provincial or, later, state concern were unanimous or nearly unanimous with extraordinary frequency. This unified expression of political ideas often went beyond the simple process of voting. The returns from the towns after votes on the Constitutions of 1778 and 1780, for example, included detailed criticisms and suggestions, and each of these was phrased as the sense of the town, which indeed it was.[81]

Provincial politics were shaped by the town. Colonists believed that political life should follow parochial norms.[82] In New England, the town was legally the basic unit of political representation, and it remained so in Massachusetts until the constitutional revisions of 1857.[83] When the "eighteenth century Yankee reflected on government," observes Robert Gross, "he thought first of his town," but this orientation to politics was not unique to New England. No less a political authority than James Madison of Virginia remarked that the "spirit of *locality*" was at the base of eighteenth-century American political culture.[84]

The persistence of community in the eighteenth century is also apparent in the ways in which religious diversity was absorbed into the organic social relations of the town. By 1760, fifty-four percent of the total population of Massachusetts (45 percent of the rural population) lived in towns with permanent dissenting congregations. Taking a different measure and a slightly later date, we can say that, in 1775, one-third of the towns in Massachusetts had at least one dissenting church.[85] The sectarian rhetoric that characterized provincial and imperial politics seems to provide ample evidence that local life had become hopelessly fragmented, but such

81. Handlin and Handlin, *Popular Sources of Political Authority*, pp. 202–323, 475–930. See also Hall, *Politics without Parties*, p. 92.

82. Waters, *Otis Family*, chap. 9; Bonomi, "Local Government in Colonial New York"; Isaac, "Dramatizing the Ideology of the Revolution."

83. Pole, *Political Representation*, pp. 38–54. See also Wood, *Creation of the American Republic*, p. 186.

84. Gross, *Minutemen and Their World*, p. 10; Madison is quoted in Wood, *Creation of the American Republic*, p. 195.

85. Murrin, "Review Essay," p. 248; Cappon, ed., *Atlas of Early American History*, p. 37. In the middle colonies, one-half of the towns had more than one denomination (ibid., p. 38).

was not the case. The lesson to be learned here is that local communities can, in an important way, contain a social life that is distinct from the provincial society of which they are a part. Close studies of local communities in New England and the middle colonies reveal that multiple sects were not incompatible with a unified community.[86] Informal and intimate patterns of social relations bridged those abstract theological differences that assumed great importance in the rhetoric of provincial politics.

In Connecticut, for example, political ideologies at the provincial level found focus in hostility to Anglicanism and to the threat of institutional intrusion through the Society for the Propagation of the Gospel in Foreign Parts or the establishment of an Anglican bishopric in the colonies. Not surprisingly, no Anglican won colonywide office. On the local level, however, one finds an intriguing surprise. Bruce Steiner has shown that Anglicans were frequently elected to important positions within the town where kin and long-established friendship ties crossed theological divisions. The advent of religious diversity, he concludes, "did not permanently disturb the most basic rhythms and deepest bonds of community life." The experience of Tories in most American communities (though not in the cities) during the Revolution provides a similar example. Informal mechanisms of social life maintained town unity. The number of Tories was always small, and their presence caused less social division within the town than party membership would a century later.[87]

86. Edmund M. Cook, Jr., *Fathers of the Towns: Leadership and Community Structure in Eighteenth Century New England* (Baltimore: Johns Hopkins, 1976), pp. 134–141; Dennis Ryan, "Six Towns: Continuity and Change in Revolutionary New Jersey, 1770–1792" (Ph.D. diss., New York University, 1974), p. 53; and Bruce Steiner, "Anglican Officeholding in Pre-Revolutionary Connecticut: The Parameters of New England Community," *WMQ*, 31 (1974): 369–406.

87. Ibid., p. 406. On Tories, see Cook, *Fathers of the Towns*, p. 189; Gross, *Minutemen and Their World*, pp. 137–138, 167–168; John A. Schutz, "Those Who Became Tories: Town Loyalty and Revolution in New England," *New England Historical and Genealogical Register*, 129 (1975), 94–105. For discussions of conflict in the cities, see Arthur M. Schlesinger, *The Colonial Merchants and the American Revolution* (New York: Atheneum, 1968); Edmund S. Morgan and Helen M. Morgan, *The Stamp Act Crisis* (Chapel Hill: University of North Carolina, 1953); and Pauline Maier, *From Resistence to Revolution* (New York: Knopf, 1972).

This evidence, which reveals a marked dissonance between local *social patterns* and translocal *ideology*, suggests that in fact two cultural systems were coexisting in the British colonies. One was a localistic oral culture based upon intimate, face-to-face relations, while the other was abstract, general, and based on the written word. One pattern of solidarity was popular, and the other was based on a formal tradition in the custody of the elite. The task of cultural leadership was to bridge these two patterns, and there is evidence that preachers of the middle eighteenth century, for example, successfully spoke to the pace and style of a shared local culture while extending this perspective to larger intellectual concerns.[88] Perhaps this is an important, if unnoticed, dimension of the Great Awakening.

The problem for the historian of community is to explore the nature of the interplay between these two cultural patterns. It may be useful in this respect to adopt the analytic distinction devised by Robert Redfield to describe the two dimensions of culture in all premodern societies: the "Little Tradition" and the "Great Tradition." The local community, which Redfield sees as the locus of the "Little Tradition," might be characterized as a "half culture" which is completed by the other half culture, the "Great Tradition." This tradition is identified with the metropolis and the intellectual elite in touch with it.[89]

For the colonial American context, this might be phrased in terms of local and provincial cultures. Within this framework, we would want answers to several questions: How do the two interact? Does each have its own world view?[90] Who is involved in each?[91] How

88. See Daniel Calhoun, *The Intelligence of a People* (Princeton: Princeton University, 1973), pp. 212, 214, 229–230.

89. See Robert Redfield, *Peasant Society and Culture* (Chicago: University of Chicago, 1956), chap. 3. See also Robert Redfield and Milton Singer, "The Cultural Role of Cities," *Economic Development and Cultural Change*, 3 (1954): 53–73.

90. Mary Douglas, in *Natural Symbols: Explorations in Cosmology* (New York: Pantheon, 1970), pp. 141–142, suggests that different kinds of social structures, plausibly equivalent to these two, produce different cosmologies.

91. An impressive beginning has been made along these lines by Cook, *Fathers of the Towns;* Isaac, "Dramatizing the Ideology of the Revolution"; and, for the special case of America's few large cities, Eric Foner, in *Tom Paine and Revolutionary America* (New York: Oxford University Press, 1976).

does this cultural complexity affect the problem of political leader-ship? It appears, for example, that the popular leaders of the Revolution, Patrick Henry in Virginia, Tom Paine in Philadelphia, and Samuel Adams in Massachusetts, were able to link these two cultural styles in their public lives.[92]

What function does one cultural system perform for the other? For instance, it seems likely that one of the ways in which local unity was preserved was by defining matters that involved conflict as translocal or provincial issues.[93] It is plausible for the towns to have used the province to achieve their traditional ends, rather than the other way around, inasmuch as the perceived needs of the towns seem to have received priority in the eighteenth century. The towns, it appears, were at the center of gravity in the political culture of the eighteenth century.[94]

The Revolutionary Era

The social sources of the American Revolution were many and complex. One that concerns us here, however, was an effort to restore communal unity that was perceived to be in danger. When Britain inaugurated the changes in imperial policy that ultimately led to the war for independence, community life in America was in crisis. Attitudes toward authority had been unsettled at least since the Great Awakening, and the practical task of maintaining communal unity was thus complicated. Towns, moreover, were running out of land; they found it difficult to provide the rising generation with a farm. This produced deep tensions and generational con-

92. On Henry, see Rhys Isaac, "Preachers and Patriots: Popular Culture and the Revolution in Virginia," in *The American Revolution: Explorations in the History of American Radicalism*, ed. Alfred Young (DeKalb: Northern Illinois University, 1976), pp. 153–154; on Paine, see Foner, *Tom Paine;* and on Adams, see Pauline Maier, *Popular Leaders of the American Revolution* (New York: New York University Press, forthcoming).

93. This is suggested by Murrin, "Review Essay," p. 256.

94. Government authority over Massachusetts towns declined in the eighteenth century. See Pole, *Political Representation,* p. 53; Zuckerman, *Peaceable Kingdoms,* chap. 1. The same may have been true in other colonies, though Ehrlich denies it in "A Town Study in Colonial New York."

flict.[95] These problems in the economic and religious dimensions of community life did not suddenly break the community apart; community now survived in spite of powerful religious and economic forces contrary to it. This tension was new to local cultures accustomed to having politics, religion, family, and the economy all reenforce each other and the town's unity.

The revolutionary crisis offered Americans an opportunity to rededicate themselves to the traditional ideals of community: love, unity, and virtue. It also focused rising feelings of aggression on an external object. Begun in pursuit of purity and the revitalization of the old, the revolutionary movement ended, paradoxically, by strengthening and formalizing social developments that ultimately transformed the structure and meaning of community in the nineteenth century.[96]

Whatever its imperial character, as an event in American social history, the American Revolution was, to borrow a phrase from Clifford Geertz, an "integrative revolution." It brought local, communal units of life, what Geertz calls "primordial groups," into relation with a national civil state.[97] We know very little about the process whereby parochial political perspectives were integrated into a national political culture, yet two developments were clearly involved: the establishment of new institutional patterns and the creation of a unifying republican ideology.[98]

The social experience of revolution and the resulting institutional innovations extended the perspective of townspeople. Using Massa-

95. See Bushman, *From Puritan to Yankee;* Edwin G. Burrows and Michael Wallace, "The American Revolution: The Ideology and Psychology of National Liberation," *Perspectives in American History,* 6 (1972): 165–306; James Henretta, *The Evolution of American Society, 1700–1851* (Lexington, Mass.: Heath, 1973); Kenneth Lockridge, "Social Change and the Meaning of the American Revolution," *JSH,* 6 (1973): 403–439; and Gross, *Minutemen and Their World,* chap. 4.

96. See ibid.; Edmund S. Morgan, "The Puritan Ethic and the American Revolution," *WMQ,* 24 (1967): 3–43; Wood, *Creation of the American Republic.*

97. Clifford Geertz, "The Integrative Revolution: Primordial Sentiments and Civil Politics in New States," in *Old Societies and New States,* ed. Clifford Geertz (New York: Free Press, 1963), pp. 154–155.

98. The former has been stressed by Richard D. Brown and the latter by John Higham. See Brown, "The Emergence of Urban Society in Rural Massachusetts," *JAH,* 61 (1974): 29–51; and Higham, "Hanging Together."

chusetts as a case for his study, Richard D. Brown demonstrates that
the Revolution brought members of town after town into association
with a broader social movement. This development altered for them
the meaning of the town by multiplying the nodes of social experience that gave structure to their lives. In addition to their older
roles as members of concentric rings of family, church, and town,
the people of Massachusetts now found themselves involved in associations and activities extending beyond the town. The revolutionary committees of correspondence initiated this pattern; in time,
additional activities developed. Men and women began to experience the "organizational variety, heterogeneity, cosmopolitanism"
once peculiar to Boston, the colony's metropolis.[99] They felt solidarity with other "patriots" as well as with fellow townsmen. They
became members of a "nation," and a bit later, they found an ex-
panding associational life. If the improvement societies that
flowered in town after town immediately following the Revolution
energized and enlivened local life, they also formalized what had
been informal, and to the degree that such clubs and associations
were exclusive, they objectified social boundaries that had pre-
viously been blurred in the interest of unity. This is especially clear
in politics where partisan divisions tended to follow existing fissures
in local communities that had earlier been played down. The party
conflicts of the 1790s brought these to the surface and accented
them.[100]

It is difficult to assess the consequences these developments had
for community. The multiplication of identities and roles, particularly the addition of translocal sources of personal orientation, undoubtedly made the traditional groups of family, church, and town
less prescriptive, making it easier to pursue the economic opportunity that beckoned elsewhere.[101] With more roles available, men
and women were more able to choose their own social identities, yet

99. Brown, "Emergence of Urban Society," p. 36.
100. See Gross, *Minutemen and Their World*, p. 174, and James H. Robbins, "The
Impact of the First American Party System on Salem Politics," *Essex Institute Historical Collections*, 107 (1971): 259–260.
101. What population and migration data are available show an upsurge of
migration in the 1790s. See Herman R. Friis, "A Series of Population Maps of the
Colonies of the United States, 1625–1790," *Geographical Review*, 30 (1940): 470.

the very process that made such choices possible brought a new rigidity to role and institutional definitions and, in turn, a restrictiveness that marked important limits to the release from traditional patterns of role acceptance.[102]

An important societal shift had occurred, one that transformed the relationship of localism to those broader social networks formerly known only to a narrow elite within the town. "Localism and insularity," Brown writes, "were being challenged, if not actually destroyed. People remained bound to the old organizations of family, church, and town, but they now possessed additional ties, links that brought them outside their family, neighborhood, and congregation and into contact with strangers."[103] The revolutionary crisis brought together the center and the periphery, local communities and fledgling structures of a national society and government, and this experience portended much for the future of community in America.

One must be careful, however, not to exaggerate the shift that actually occurred between 1750 and, say, 1820. Henry Adams's portrait of parochialism and isolation in 1800 remains compelling.[104] If the psychological and institutional bonds of the local community were less confining and people were more mobile, the town remained, nevertheless, the primary orientation of social life for its members. The spirit of American localism was captured by an English visitor to America who, in 1807, observed that whereas Englishmen think in terms of "Church and nation," in the United States, the typical reference is only to the "village and congregation."[105] We might say, therefore, that although Brown has located the sources of change, the changes were to take decades to material-

102. This issue remains to be studied by historians. For some theoretical beginnings, see Fred Weinstein and Gerald Platt, *The Wish To Be Free: Society, Psyche, and Value Change* (Berkeley and Los Angeles: University of California, 1969), and idem., *Psychoanalytic Sociology* (Baltimore: Johns Hopkins, 1973).

103. Brown, "Emergence of Urban Society," pp. 42–43. The process Brown finds in Massachusetts town life seem to have occurred also in Pennsylvania. See the data in Lemon, *Best Poor Man's Country*, pp. 139–140.

104. Henry Adams, *The United States in 1800* (Ithaca, N.Y.: Cornell University, 1955).

105. Gregory H. Singleton, "Protestant Voluntary Organizations and the Shaping of Victorian America," *AQ*, 27 (1975): 551.

ize fully. The institutional paths he found leading out of the town were still faint traces that only later would become heavily trod byways. Robert Wiebe's characterization of the early national period as one of "triumphant particularism" rings true.[106]

While the institutional changes noted by Brown were occurring, Americans were beginning to identify with the republican ideology that emerged from the Revolution. Although ideology can create a national community held together by emotional bonds similar to those associated with the social experience of community that we are here discussing, such local and national feelings are distinct, and they are not mutually exclusive commitments. The Revolutionary ideology, although it was an important source of national cohesion, did not draw Americans out of their basically communal orientation to life, nor did it call forth a national *society*. Rather, it linked diverse local communities that collectively formed the nation.[107]

Much of the literature on social and political mobilization in contemporary developing nations suggests that identities based upon shared national ideologies replaced primordial sources of identity destroyed by modernization. The process in the United States seems to have been more complex.[108] Americans apparently felt no contradiction in combining a fervent belief in republicanism, defined by abstract ideals of liberty and virtue, with a deep attachment to the local community.

Eighteenth-century American political theory, we might recall, made an important distinction between society and the state. The state in the eighteenth century, in contrast to the twentieth, was not deeply embedded in daily social experiences, for society and state were sharply distinguished. Whereas the state, or the government, operated through formal and often alien institutions that could be

---

106. Wiebe, *Segmented Society,* p. 36.
107. On the role of ideology, see Higham, "Hanging Together."
108. For a major statement of the conventional view, see Karl W. Deutsch, "Social Mobilization and Political Development," *APSR,* 55 (1961): 493–514. The complexity I see in the United States seems to find a parallel in nineteenth-century France. See Eugen Weber, *Peasants into Frenchmen* (Stanford: Stanford University, 1976), p. 113.

used to coerce the population, society was conceived in communal terms: small in scale, personal, and unified.[109]

The genius of the Constitutional Convention was that it produced a radically new frame of national government that stopped short of a revolution in social organization. Some centralization was achieved, yet local communities retained their integrity as social and political units. The constitutional resolution of 1789 combined two political cultures, one formal and contractual, the other essentially communal. Viewed as the "reform" of a national elite dissatisfied with the Articles of Confederation, the elitist and centralizing character of the Constitution is clear.[110] The men who drafted it spoke for a "Great Tradition" of politics that was somewhat detached from local communities, and the political structure they created, reflecting this tradition, was liberal rather than communal.[111] It envisioned a politics of conflicting interests that would be moderated by a translocal political elite. This was an innovation for Americans used to a politics that was, as with the ancient Greeks, fundamentally face-to-face and local. With the advent of the Constitution, Americans did not abandon this pattern of politics; they became involved in two political cultures.

The Constitution fell far short of consolidation. There was ample space in the newly created *state* for the communities that constituted the basic units of life in American *society*, communities that nourished a "Little Tradition" celebrating informal and consensual politics. This political style provided the basis for the anti-Federalist fear that the Constitution would replace communal politics with a consolidated government detached from the texture of local life.

109. Sheldon Wolin, *Politics and Vision: Continuity and Innovation in Western Political Thought* (Boston: Little, Brown, 1960), p. 130. See also Michael P. Rogin, *Fathers and Children: Andrew Jackson and the Subjugation of the American Indian* (New York: Knopf, 1975), p. 26. The sociological significance of this issue is considered by Norman Birnbaum, *The Crisis of Industrial Society* (New York: Oxford University Press, 1969), pp. 34–35.

110. See Wood, *Creation of the American Republic.*

111. On this distinction in political theory and in historical practice, see Benjamin R. Barber, *The Death of Communal Liberty: A History of Freedom in a Swiss Mountain Canton* (Princeton: Princeton University, 1974).

Imagining only a unitary model of politics, the anti-Federalists assumed that any larger polity would be an extension of the local political cultures they knew, and they realized that a politics based upon face-to-face relationships could not work on the scale contemplated by the writers of the Constitution.[112] Their first assumption being wrong, however, caused them to fear the Constitution more than they need have. Their fears proved groundless, at least in the short run. The settlement of 1789 produced not a unitary, but a dual, political culture. It comprehended both the old and a new pattern of politics.

An informal, communal, and essentially oral politics continued to flourish at the local level, while at the national level, and to some degree at the state levels, a formal system, abstracted from society, accepted conflict and majoritarianism in a way that was alien to local political cultures.[113] If the local political cultures based upon shared social experience remained largely customary and trusting, the national one was contractual in the modern sense and relied upon precise articulation of rights and duties—in writing, as in the case of the Bill of Rights.[114]

The political impulse toward a purer and more homogeneous community that had prevailed at the beginning of the revolutionary crisis had been transformed into a political system that combined many small and personal local political units with one large and abstract one.[115] The degree of interpenetration was minimal; a doctrine of spheres seems to have prevailed. This division was apparent a generation later when de Tocqueville observed what

112. On the political theory of the anti-Federalists, see Cecelia M. Kenyon, "Men of Little Faith: The Anti-Federalists on the Nature of Representative Government," *WMQ*, 12 (1955): 3–46. On the distinction between face-to-face and modern politics, see Peter Laslett, "The Face to Face Society," in *Philosophy, Politics and Society*, ed. Peter Laslett (Oxford: Blackwell, 1967), pp. 157–184.

113. See James Madison, *Federalist*, no. 10.

114. Wiebe, *Segmented Society*, p. 15. See also Calhoun, *Intelligence of a People*, p. 332.

115. Where the states relate to all of this is not entirely clear. There has been too little research on them to make any confident assessment, but they seem to represent a version of the abstract model.

seemed to him were two political systems in America: "the one fulfilling the ordinary duties and responding to the daily and infinite calls of a community, the other circumscribed within certain limits and exercising an exceptional authority over the general interests of the country."[116]

When Hamilton had sought in the 1790s to create out of the materials provided by the Constitution a powerful national government independent of the little communities sprinkled over the American landscape, Americans were frightened, and he failed. Jefferson's successful response may have been misty and vague (and in retrospect therefore vulnerable), but it assured the people that identification with American nationalism was compatible with the web of community that bounded their primary social experience,[117] and for several decades after 1789 local elites, as local elites, continued to shape public policy.[118] Within the new framework of national government, public affairs were placed primarily in the hands of leaders whose authority was grounded upon their status in local units of life. Not until the impulse toward centralization associated with the Civil War, which can, after all, be interpreted as a war of national unification, was the character of the revolutionary settlement fundamentally altered.[119]

116. Alexis de Tocqueville, *Democracy in America*, 2 vols. (New York: Random House, Vintage, 1945), 1:61–62.

117. See Rowland Berthoff and John Murrin, "Feudalism, Communalism, and the Yeoman Freeholder: The American Revolution Considered as a Social Accident," in *Essays on the American Revolution* ed. Stephen Kurtz and James Hutson (Chapel Hill: University of North Carolina, 1973), p. 288; Wiebe, *Segmented Society*, pp. 101–102; Robert Kelley, *The Transatlantic Persuasion: The Liberal-Democratic Mind in the Age of Gladstone* (New York: Knopf, 1969), pp. 129–131.

118. See, for example, Oscar Handlin and Mary Handlin, *Commonwealth*; Richard Wade, *The Urban Frontier* (Chicago: University of Chicago, 1964); James Willard Hurst, *Law and the Conditions of Freedom in the Nineteenth Century United States* (Madison: University of Wisconsin, 1956); and Thomas Bender, "Law, Economy, and Social Values in Jacksonian America: A Maryland Case Study," *Maryland Historical Magazine*, 71 (1976): 484–497.

119. On the Civil War, I am referring primarily to the observation of Allan Nevins, *The War for the Union*, 4 vols. (New York: Scribner's, 1959–1971), 1:v. See also David Potter, "Civil War," in *The Comparative Approach to American History*, ed. C. Vann Woodward (New York: Basic, 1968), pp. 135–145.

The Mid-nineteenth Century

For two decades following the ratification of the Constitution, American society seems to have regressed into a stolid communalism.[120] After the War of 1812, however, there became apparent a new dynamism perhaps best symbolized by the acceleration of the movement west. Morris Birkbeck, an English visitor, remarked in 1817 that "Old America seems to be breaking up, and moving westward."[121] Demographic data bear out Birkbeck's observation, yet his statement, with its hint of community decline, invites misinterpretation. The movement he describes is not necessarily incompatible with a persistence of community as an American ideal and as a widespread experience.

The local community left by the migrants, especially that in New England, remained knitted together by family and friendship networks well into the nineteenth century. Timothy Dwight, writing as the eighteenth century passed into the nineteenth, observed that a "general spirit of good neighborhood" and of mutual aid were "part of the established manners" of New England's towns.[122] Migrants, typically motivated by economic pressures, may have left the town of their birth, but they did not reject the idea that life was properly lived in bounded local communities. They had internalized this value, and they carried it with them.[123]

Although Americans continued to act out their lives within the context of the town, the town and the experience of community took on a new quality after about 1820. These changes made the nine-

120. There is not a specific study on this point, but there are hints of it in several. See, for example, Berthoff and Murrin, "Feudalism, Communalism, and the Yeoman Freeholder," and Adams, *The United States in 1800*.

121. Quoted in Frederick Jackson Turner, *Rise of the New West, 1819–1829* (New York: Macmillan [Collier], 1962), p. 72.

122. Bash, "Factors Influencing Family and Community Organization," pp. 31–35, 185–186, 210–211, and Timothy Dwight, *Travels in New England and New-York*, 4 vols. (1821–1822), 1:468. For an evocation of life in a New England town around 1830, see the autobiographical account in Charles Capen McLaughlin, ed., *The Papers of Frederick Law Olmsted*, 1 vol. to date (Baltimore: Johns Hopkins, 1977), 1:100–103.

123. See Smith, *As a City upon a Hill*.

teenth-century town, as a locus of community, increasingly different from its eighteenth-century counterpart. Writing late in the nineteenth century from the perspective of Quincy, Massachusetts, Charles Francis Adams, Jr., noted that during these years "the period of immobility and sameness had come to an end." For him, the symbol of this change was the development of the quarry at Quincy to supply granite for a growing Boston. "Its influence," Adams wrote, "was everywhere felt,—in habits and modes of life and thought, and in politics." Adams may have exaggerated the sameness and the static quality of an earlier Quincy, but he captured a fundamental truth in his realization that something connected with larger economic and political structures produced a change in local life that "was felt not only everywhere, but in all sorts of ways."[124]

The emerging national economic system, together with the increased mobility made possible in part by improvements in transportation, with national political parties, and with other regional and national voluntary associations, brought a new configuration to local life. Although the first impulse of the historian and social scientist is to describe this transformation as an eclipse of local life by larger and more important social aggregates, something different seems actually to have happened. The initial consequence of nationalism and metropolitanism was, as Stuart Blumin and Richard Birdsall have shown, an enhancement of local identifications. However paradoxical it may appear, nationalism and localism as basic orientations to life were simultaneously enhanced, and in some respects they even reenforced each other during the first half of the nineteenth century.[125]

During the ages of Jackson and Lincoln, American nationalism

124. Charles Francis Adams, Jr., *Three Episodes of Massachusetts History*, 2 vols. (Boston: Houghton Mifflin, 1892), 2:927–928.

125. See Stuart Blumin, *The Urban Threshold: Growth and Change in a Nineteenth-Century American Community* (Chicago: University of Chicago, 1976), and Richard Birdsall, *Berkshire County: A Cultural History* (New Haven: Yale University, 1959). At the same time that the nation's major metropolises were extending their influence, smaller cities, with their own strong identities, were filling out the national urban network. See Michael P. Conzen, "Metropolitan Dominance in the American Midwest during the Later Nineteenth Century" (Ph.D. diss., University of Wisconsin, 1972).

was founded upon a few national orthodoxies that provided vehicles for individual identification with the nation. The vast majority of Americans shared beliefs in American national superiority, Protestantism, democracy, the racial supremacy of whites, and the value of free labor and enterprise. Some Americans, of course, dissented from these notions and still others were victims of them, but such conflict actually strengthened the hold of these ideologies.[126] By the eve of the Civil War, these ideologies and feelings of nationhood had come to center on the idea of Union. This notion, so central to the thought and politics of Lincoln, had, in the words of Owen Lovejoy, a radical congressman from Illinois, become "a holy instrument around which all American hearts cluster and to which they cling with the tenacity of a semi-religious attachment."[127]

If Americans, both northerners and southerners each in their own way, thus felt a kind of spiritual unity that made for a sense of national community at mid-century, this nationalism had little institutional reality.[128] Mid-century American nationalism, almost like the sense of being a Greek at the time of Socrates, was a deeply held abstraction. By contrast, the local community, like the polis, was a concrete reality that was immediately seen, felt, and experienced. To the extent that nationalism was given tangible form, it was in this local and immediate context. These local manifestations of nationalism, whether Fourth of July orations or other patriotic rituals, had the effect of enhancing the solidarity of the local community.

Under the broad umbrella of American nationalism, between

126. On these ideologies, see Charles L. Sanford, *The Quest for Paradise: Europe and the American Moral Imagination* (Urbana: University of Illinois, 1961); Sidney Mead, *The Lively Experiment: The Shaping of Christianity in America* (New York: Harper, 1963); Perry Miller, *The Life of the Mind in America* (New York: Harcourt, 1965); Irving Bartlett, *The American Mind in the Mid-Nineteenth Century* (New York: Crowell, 1967); Ralph Gabriel, *The Course of American Democratic Thought*, 2d ed. (New York: Ronald, 1956), pt. I; George Fredrickson, *The Black Image in the White Mind* (New York: Harper, 1971); Higham, "Hanging Together"; and Eric Foner, *Free Soil, Free Labor and Free Men* (New York: Oxford University Press, 1970).

127. Quoted in Paul C. Nagel, *One Nation Indivisible: The Union in American Thought, 1776–1861* (New York: Oxford University Press, 1964), p. 9.

128. See David Potter, *History and American Society*, chaps. 4–5.

about 1820 and 1870, society was remarkably decentralized. The local units of life were replicated across the landscape. If nearly all Americans subscribed to a relatively small number of common beliefs, they also tended to live in local communities that took pride in their parochialism and idiosyncratic ways. Each village and town, de Tocqueville observed, "forms a sort of republic, accustomed to govern itself."[129] The outside world constantly intruded—more so than in the ages of Washington and Jefferson—but a local perspective predominated. According to Daniel Aaron, writing with respect to Cincinnati in the 1820s and 1830s, local responsibilities "enveloped the individual citizen."[130]

Each town had its own pattern of local values independent of national ones, though not in conflict with them. These local values, typically in the custodianship of the local elite, could vary significantly from town to town, and these differences could mean distinctive social experiences.[131] The common denominator of local life was, however, the experience of community. Role performance and status at the local level were differentiated from one's role as a national citizen, and the boundaries of most social roles coincided with the local community.[132] Certainly the sense of belonging to a local community was less intense than that characteristic of earlier Puritan towns, yet one finds social ideals and economic interest threaded through the town in a way that was sufficient to weave a fabric of community to wrap around the local social experience.[133]

Social and cultural categories were basically the same in town

129. Quoted in Stuart Bruchey, *The Roots of American Economic Growth, 1607–1861* (New York: Harper, 1965), p. 94.

130. Daniel Aaron, "Cincinnati, 1818–1838" (Ph.D. diss., Harvard, 1943), p. 201.

131. Richard S. Alcorn, "Leadership and Stability in Mid-Nineteenth Century America: A Case Study of an Illinois Town," *JAH*, 61 (1974): 686.

132. On the conceptual issues implied here, see Yehudi A. Cohen, "Social Boundary Systems," *Current Anthropology*, 10 (1969): 103–126, and Bernard Barber, "Family Status, Local-Community Status, and Social Stratification: Three Types of Social Ranking," *Pacific Sociological Review*, 4 (1961): 3–10.

133. See Wade, *Urban Frontier*; Daniel Boorstin, *The Americans: The National Experience* (New York: Random House, Vintage, 1965), bk. I; Aaron, "Cincinnati," p. 489; Stanley Elkins and Eric McKitrick, "A Meaning for Turner's Frontier," *Political Science Quarterly*, 59 (1954): 321–353, 565–602.

after town, but it would be a mistake to interpret this as a manifestation of metropolitan culture. There were no agreed-upon and accepted social and cultural standards radiating out of the metropolis. Each town took conventional social categories from the metropolis and reformulated them in local terms, and each town treated its system of status in its own terms as well. The effect was an alteration of conventional roles that occurred in the process of fitting local figures into them. If the general character of the status system was evident in town after town, still, it was treated locally as an autonomous system. This approach to social categories is apparent in DeWitt Clinton's 1822 observations on New York State:

> In cities, towns, and villages, the leading members of the learned professions, the principal merchants and agriculturists, form a distinct association. . . . In the middle ranks in villages, the bar keeper is an important personage and so is the mistress of the school, who is generally a well educated, well-behaved young woman. They set the fashions for their associates, and give tone to opinion. In some places the stage-driver is a leading beau, and the keeper of the turnpike gate is a man of consequence.[134]

Social status was linked to the local human surround that provided the context for one's life. Hence there was really no single scale upon which individuals from several towns could be ranked. One town and its leaders might be richer, economically or culturally, than another, but Americans in the early nineteenth century found it difficult, if they tried at all, to describe relative social status across space. Institutional connections were too fragile for this; besides, as we shall presently see, what translocal institutions did exist served to reenforce localistic patterns of identification even while they provided rough general standards for assessing personal character.

In cultural life, one finds the same pattern of localism. All towns, even very small ones, tried to establish and support a full range of cultural institutions: newspaper, museum, learned society, hotel,

---

134. [DeWitt Clinton], *Letters on the Natural History and Internal Resources of the State of New York* (New York: Bliss and White, 1822), pp. 56–58.

and college. Although these institutions tended to have remarkably wide community participation, they also largely abandoned any attempt to maintain a uniform or metropolitan set of cultural standards. Daniel Drake, a leader in early Cincinnati's cultural life, justified this pattern in a speech he delivered in 1814. "Learning, philosophy and taste," he observed, "are yet in early infancy" in Cincinnati and "the standard of excellence in literature and science is proportionably low." Yet he insisted that cultural achievement could be viewed legitimately from a local perspective and need not be intimidated by cosmopolitan standards:

> Those who attain to superiority in the community of which they are members, are relatively great. Literary excellence in Paris, London, Edinburgh is *incomparable* with the same thing in Philadelphia, New York or Boston: while each of these, in turn, has a standard of merit, which may be contrasted, but cannot be compared, with that of Lexington or Cincinnati.[135]

Institutions of higher education identified with communities, always defined in terms of a spiritual flock, often in terms of the immediate locality. Williams College, for example, was completely representative of life in Berkshire County at mid century. Mark Hopkins, president of the institution from 1836 to 1872, made this point in his inaugural address: "I have no ambition to build up here what would be called a great institution. The wants of the community do not require it." The spiritual and territorial definitions of the college's community here coincided. The moral constituency of colleges and the financial resources vital to their success were not always locality based, but very often were.[136]

135. Henry D. Shapiro and Zane L. Miller, eds., *Physician to the West: Selected Writings of Daniel Drake on Science and Society* (Lexington: University of Kentucky, 1970), p. 59. For a fuller discussion of this point, see Thomas Bender, "Science and the Culture of American Communities: The Nineteenth Century," *HEQ*, 16 (1976): 63–77.

136. Hopkins is quoted in Birdsall, *Berkshire County*, p. 145n. For the best case study of this issue, see Marilyn Tobias, "Old Dartmouth on Trial: The Transformation of the Academic Community in Nineteenth-Century America" (Ph.D. diss., New York University, 1977). See also David Potts, "College Enthusiasm as Public Response, 1800–1860," *HER*, 47 (1977): 28–42.

Local ministers were largely isolated from the status-giving context of the church. The minister derived his status from face-to-face contact with the lay people who made up his congregation. In this situation, character was more important than metropolitan standards of learning. Lyman Beecher put the point well when he observed: "Each pastor stands upon his own character and deeds, without anything to break the force of his responsibility to his people."[137] The reputation of physicians seems also to have rested upon a trust that was based upon personal acquaintance rather than upon scientific expertise meeting metropolitan standards.[138]

This impressionistic evidence pointing toward the persistence of a community orientation is plausible in its own terms, but what about recent quantitative findings regarding geographic mobility? One of the most important substantive contributions of the new urban and social history has been the discovery of extraordinarily high levels of geographic mobility at least since the 1820s. With about one-third of the population of towns disappearing between decadal censuses, how could any semblance of community be preserved?[139]

Two things, one already noted in another connection, need to be said here. The mere fact of moving does not necessarily imply an atomized society. In fact, nineteenth-century Americans moved from *community* to *community*. That these communities were constructed, so to speak, on the spot, does not make them any less communal. Even the intense Puritan communities of the seventeenth century were, we might recall, like a good marriage—a social

137. Sidney Mead, "The Rise of the Evangelical Conception of the Ministry in America, 1607–1850," in *The Ministry in Historical Perspectives*, ed. H. Richard Niebuhr and Daniel Williams (New York: Harper, 1956), pp. 212–218, quotation from p. 218. Cf. Calhoun, *Professional Lives*, pp. 116–117, 152–157, 169–171.

138. Donald Fleming, *William H. Welch and the Rise of Modern Medicine* (Boston: Little, Brown, 1954), p. 22; William R. Johnson, "Education and Professional Life-styles: Law and Medicine in the Nineteenth Century," *HEQ*, 14 (1974): 185–208.

139. This question is posed in one of the earliest and best of these studies, Stephan Thernstrom and Peter Knights, "Men in Motion: Some Data and Speculations about Urban Population Mobility in Nineteenth Century America," *JIH*, 1 (1970): 7–35. Its initial quantitative findings have been essentially sustained in subsequent studies too numerous to cite here.

construction, not something made in heaven or dependent upon
some prior mystical bond. Secondly, some Americans moved more
than others. There were apparently two populations in nineteenth-
century towns, an economically successful permanent group who
shaped the values and direction of social life in the town, and a
floating, largely unsuccessful group.[140] We know little about those
who left nineteenth-century towns. They may have drifted through
American society without ever finding economic success or without
forming an attachment with any local community, or they may
eventually have found a town that offered the economic opportunity
and life-style they sought.

The successful, whatever their route to this success, typically
identified with the town that gave them their success—and their
status. By contrast, in the late twentieth century, this connection
between success and local status has been severed. That career lines,
professions, and national economic and political institutions, not
localities, confer economic success is apparent in the changing
pattern of social and geographic mobility.[141] In contemporary
America, men and women do not so much move from one town to
another as follow an advantageous career path that may take them
to a number of basically incidental locations.[142] The mid-nineteenth century was radically different; men and women passed
through various professions or career lines as they moved from community to community.[143]

140. See Michael B. Katz, *The People of Hamilton, Canada West* (Cambridge:
Harvard University, 1975), p. 21; Kenneth MacLeish and Kimball Young, *Culture of
a Contemporary Rural Community: Landaff, New Hampshire* (Washington D.C.:
U.S. Department of Agriculture, 1942), p. 6; Bash, "Factors Influencing Family and
Community Organization," p. 175.

141. See Stephan Thernstrom, *The Other Bostonians: Poverty and Progress in the
American Metropolis* (Cambridge: Harvard University, 1973), p. 42.

142. Perhaps the same can be said of the poor of the mid-twentieth century, who
pursue the most advantageous path of welfare benefits, for largely the same reasons.

143. According to the OED, it was in 1868 that the word *career* was first used to
signify a course of professional progress or advancement in employment. My colleague
Paul Mattingly informs me, however, that this usage appears well before this date. It
was used by Horace Mann in his advice book, *Thoughts for a Young Man* (1850).
Whatever the precise dating on the first usage of the term, *careers* in this sense probably did not represent a widespread social experience until the last decade or so of

If the mobility that looms so large in recent historiography is, after all, compatible with identifications based upon the local community, what about the transportation revolution, the emergence of a nationally integrated economy, and the development of regional and national organizations? Contrary to expectation, local life did not lose its vitality immediately and directly. The configuration of community was clearly affected, but its locality base was not destroyed.

Some years ago, in a fascinating if idiosyncratic study of Berkshire County, Richard Birdsall suggested that the first effect of metropolitanism was to intensify localism. If, in the long run, the intrusion of metropolitan influences eroded the significance of the local community, the result in the short run was an impressive invigoration of local life in Berkshire County.[144] More recently, Stuart Blumin, apparently unaware of Birdsall's work, asked a similar question in respect to the Hudson River town of Kingston, New York: What happened to local communities in the era of the transportation revolution and growing nationalism? He found that between 1820 and 1860 the significance of place did not decline in Kingston. Indeed, people's lives were oriented toward the local community with more intensity in 1860 than in 1820. He concludes that "the creation of a nationally integrated economy and society," with its various agencies of nonlocal social organization, "did not *simply* create a national consciousness among Americans. By vitalizing secondary urban centers, it also created a countercurrent of parochial, community-based action and identity."[145]

Religious institutions—the benevolence empires and the evangelical churches—helped nationalize American society during the first decades of the nineteenth century, but they did not do this through institutional centralization or at the expense of local culture. Again, the enhancement of national values and institutions occurred in

---

the nineteenth century. On the slow development of career orientations among nineteenth-century college graduates, see Colin Burke, "The Quiet Influence: American Colleges and Their Students, 1800–1860" (Ph.D., diss., Washington University, 1973), p. 145.

144. Birdsall, *Berkshire County*.
145. Blumin, *Urban Threshold*, p. 222.

tandem with the strengthening of local ones. The Second Great Awakening, for example, was a general social movement of national scope, but, as Donald G. Mathews has perceptively pointed out, rather than resulting in consolidation, it organized thousands of people into small groups. It created "strong local churches that shared common values and norms with their counterparts throughout the United States." While nationalizing American society, these religious groups, particularly Methodist and Baptist churches, were also unifying and invigorating local community life, so that this nationalizing influence was linked to intense and intimate experiences in local, small communities. "From Maine to Georgia," Mathews writes, "the people of the new nation were being recruited into the various local organizations of a vast social movement."[146]

Because American cities and towns of the mid-nineteenth century were elements of a large and complex national society, it would be an error to view them as self-contained local systems of social life. They had a genuine local existence, but they were also localized articulations of social organizations that extended beyond the community.[147] From this perspective the significance of locality must be empirically judged within a broader context. One might find that local life is completely fragmented with the local terminals of translocal social institutions not even touching at the local level. Conversely, it is equally possible to perceive the ways in which a local pattern of social relations might weave larger strands of social life into a single web of community. What evidence is available suggests that some national and regional institutions divided communities, as antislavery organizations did in the 1830s, while others facilitated the social construction of an integrated community, as the evangelical churches did during the same period.[148]

146. Donald G. Mathews, "The Second Great Awakening as an Organizing Process, 1780–1830: An Hypothesis," *AQ*, 21 (1969): 42–43, 37.

147. See Wolf, "Aspects of Group Relations in a Complex Society," pp. 1065–1078. See also Julian Steward, *Theory of Culture Change* (Urbana: University of Illinois, 1955), chap. 3.

148. Contrast the findings in Leonard L. Richards, *Gentlemen of Property and Standing: Anti-Abolition Mobs in Jacksonian America* (New York: Oxford University Press, 1970), with those in T. Scott Miyakawa, *Protestants and Pioneers: Individualism and Conformity on the American Frontier* (Chicago: University of Chicago, 1964).

Community construction during the westward movement provides an example of the way national institutions helped integrate
local communities. The westward movement is usually depicted as
lonely pioneer families making their way, but it was also a com-
munity-building process.[149] Men and women moved west in the
company of kin or friends; they were also quick to form a network of
community relations in the new localities where they settled. The
like-minded tended to find each other. Sometimes this like-minded-
ness was founded on common origins (in, for instance, Vermont or a
region of Europe); more often, membership in national institutions,
whether churches or other voluntary associations, facilitated the
development of new bonds of community.[150]

The role of churches, political parties, and other voluntary societies was crucial in the construction of communities.[151] These voluntary associations, as Michael Rogin has pointed out, were both
associational (e.g., instrumental) and communal. Men became
"brothers" in settings that mixed mutuality and communal loyalty
with self-interest. This same combination of sentiment and self-interest, incidentally, was also apparent in the ethnic associations that
emerged later in the century.[152]

On the extremely fruitful concept of the social construction of communities, see
Suttles, *Social Construction of Communities*.

149. See Elkins and McKitrick, "A Meaning for Turner's Frontier"; Boorstin,
Americans.

150. See Ronald P. Formisano, *The Birth of Mass Political Parties: Michigan,
1827–1861* (Princeton: Princeton University, 1971), pp. 167, 169; Michael P.
Conzen, *Frontier Farming in an Urban Shadow* (Madison: State Historical Society
of Wisconsin, 1971), pp. 55–60; Don H. Doyle, "Social Theory and New Communities in Nineteenth Century America" (Paper delivered at the Social Science
History Association Meeting, Madison, Wisconsin, April, 1976).

151. See the data, if not the interpretation, in Walter S. Glazer, "Participation and
Power: Voluntary Associations and the Functional Organization of Cincinnati in
1840," *HMN*, 5 (1972): 151–168.

152. See Rogin, *Fathers and Children*, p. 92, and Handlin and Handlin, *Dimensions
of Liberty*, p. 116. Josef J. Barton, *Peasants and Strangers: Italians, Rumanians and
Slovaks in an American City, 1890–1950* (Cambridge: Harvard University, 1975),
chap. 4, shows the links between sentiment and interest in ethnic organizations. This
combination is also evident in some nineteenth-century professional structures. See
Monte Calvert, *The Mechanical Engineer in America, 1830–1910* (Baltimore: Johns
Hopkins, 1967).

The way in which evangelical churches helped to integrate local community life in the West has been studied with great insight by T. Scott Miyakawa.[153] He points out that the churches provided essentially uniform standards for behavior and community participation that could be, and were, replicated in town after town in the Middle West. "To a considerable extent," he writes, "the churches were at once centers of religious and social life, advocates of public order, and schools for group and community leadership."[154] Miyakawa explains what Max Weber observed long ago when he briefly visited the United States: Membership in American churches provided newcomers who would otherwise be strangers with a "certificate of moral qualification."[155] Whereas Weber stressed the value of this in establishing business relations, Miyakawa notices how it might facilitate the process of community formation. By creating a "vital fellowship," the churches were the means through which "hitherto complete strangers" could "establish close personal relations quickly."[156] The external or translocal organization thus became the means for establishing a local solidarity group. It drew people together into a community.[157]

The socioreligious community provided an intimate core of experience in most American communities. While it is true that there were often several denominations in a town, one was usually dominant. More important perhaps, all the churches were oriented to the local community, which in turn provided the basis for well-developed ties among them. Individual citizens identified with their community through membership in intimate groups that were considerably smaller than the whole town, but with church leaders, including the minister, providing the general leadership for the

153. Miyakawa, *Protestants and Pioneers*. For a similar argument in respect to a New York town, see Stuart Blumin, "Church and Community: A Case Study of Lay Leadership in Nineteenth Century America," *New York History*, 56 (1975): 393–408.

154. Miyakawa, *Protestants and Pioneers*, p. 3.

155. H. H. Gerth and C. Wright Mills, eds., *From Max Weber* (New York: Oxford University Press, 1958), p. 305.

156. Miyakawa, *Protestants and Pioneers*, p. 214. Social clubs and academic degrees may have assumed this function later in American history.

157. Suttles argues that government programs inviting local participation perform this function in our largest cities. See his *Social Construction of Communities*.

community, commitment to smaller units did not conflict with community identification based on locality.[158] Indeed, it probably reenforced such an identity. In a social sense, the leaders of all the denominations within the Christian fold (with Catholics sometimes included even in Protestant towns) were linked together as the general moral voice of the community. The activities of the minister in this process had their counterparts in the roles assumed by teachers and college graduates migrating west.[159]

The rituals of national patriotism also enhanced the significance of local ties of community. Fourth of July celebrations, electioneering parades and festivals, and other patriotic celebrations that were conducted on the local level, by local committees, had the effect of invigorating the sense and experience of community in town after town. The process of planning such celebrations emphasized the importance of the local community. Although the ostensible purpose was national, experientially it was a communal event firmly rooted in a local context.[160]

What can be said in summary about locality's relation to community during the half century or so following 1820? It is clear that a sense of human connection coincided with the geographic boundaries of the town. The immediate human surround for people's lives was localized in the town, and, more important, it comprehended the whole town. Unfortunately, existing studies are not very precise in delineating the character of local social relationships. In

158. The role of the minister in this deserves much study. For some suggestions, see Mead, "Evangelical Conception of the Ministry in America," p. 212; Blumin, "Church and Community"; and Timothy L. Smith, "Protestant Schooling and American Nationality, 1800–1850," *JAH*, 53 (1967): 679–695.
159. Blumin, "Church and Community." For an example of Catholic churches being brought into this local network of moral leadership, see Thernstrom, *Poverty and Progress*, chap. 7. On college graduates, see Burke, "Quiet Influence," pp. 206–224 and passim. For a beginning of the sort of analysis we need of the process whereby teachers settled into communities, see David Tyack, *The One Best System* (Cambridge: Harvard University, 1974), pp. 13–21.
160. See Russo, *Families and Communities*, p. 114; Aaron, "Cincinnati," pp. 194–197.

arguing for the importance of localized social orientations, scholars have failed to specify different kinds and qualities of interactions that may have characterized these relationships. Surely not all of them qualify for our definition of community. A claim that residents of mid-nineteenth-century towns were intimately involved with or even knew everyone in the town is hardly credible.

Despite all this, the town was the most important container for the social lives of men and women, and community was found within it. Even though the literature is undependable on this point, one might speculate on the different kinds of localized social relationships that were available to people in towns in the middle of the nineteenth century. The geographic place seems to have provided a supportive human surround made up of a series of distinct relationships that can be visualized in the image of concentric circles. In earlier Puritan villages, these circles of relations had been, as we have seen, of nearly equal intensity and were highly permeable, but now, a sharp division among them was clear. The innermost ring encompassed kin, while the second represented friends who were treated as kin. Here was the core experience of community. Beyond these rings were two others: those with whom one dealt regularly and thus knew, and, finally, those people who were recognized as members of the town but who were not necessarily known.

In the town of the mid-eighteenth century, the third ring was part of the communal experience and the fourth did not exist. Shifting the comparison, it can be said that these two forms of relationship exist in the twentieth century, but with important differences. At first glance, one might see in these last two rings examples of the "community of limited liability" sociologists have detected in metropolitan neighborhoods. The notion of limited liability does describe the nature of obligation contained in these relationships; for example, they are easily severed by geographic mobility out of the town. I want, however, to stress a difference. The community of limited liability of the mid-nineteenth century was global and comprehensive, that is, it encompassed the whole town and all the activities of the town's population. There was thus a symmetry to the concentric circles—all bounded by the town—that is absent in the twentieth-century metropolis. The community of limited liability described in studies of modern neighborhoods typically comprehends only the domestic dimension of life: family life and the provision of services supportive of it. In the town of the mid-nineteenth century, however, all human activities were acted out within a context marked by a localized sense of connectedness. To an important degree, therefore, the local community of limited liability reenforced the more profound localized experience of community.

Locality, Leadership, and Politics

Although I have emphasized the integrating forces present in towns of the mid-nineteenth century, I am not arguing that there was no important political conflict in them.[161] Conflict within the bounds of the local community did become more prominent than it had been a century earlier. Not all of this conflict, however, was destructive of strong primary identifications with the local community. Local political conflicts could even enhance this identification simply because the local community, by providing an arena for conflict, can strengthen the sense of local boundedness.

The pattern of this integration in the nineteenth century differed sharply from the earlier eighteenth-century model, however; the community no longer spoke to the outside world with a single political voice. Different groups within the town sought and increasingly achieved independent access to metropolitan institutions. Traditional channels of leadership could be bypassed because innovations in communication expanded the public. But technological innovation alone did not produce the change in behavior. New ways of advancing political interests were encouraged by egalitarian ideologies and by men who could benefit by filling the new social roles implied by a more highly differentiated pattern of leadership. Before 1870, one can talk only about beginnings, but already this new pattern of

161. On this issue, compare Elkins and McKitrick, "A Meaning for Turner's Frontier," with Robert Dykstra, *The Cattle Towns* (New York: Atheneum, 1968), pp. 371–378.

access to external institutions had begun to affect the integrity of local life.[162]

The changing character of nineteenth-century local political life is difficult to trace, but surely it bears importantly on the question of community. Unfortunately, there are no nineteenth-century studies comparable to those for towns of the mid-twentieth century showing how the politics of the metropolis intrudes into local life and reveals fault lines dividing what on the surface appears to be a genuine community.[163]

Anthropologists have, however, suggested typologies of interaction that might guide our speculations concerning the nineteenth century. Relations between the center and the periphery, or the town and the metropolis, might be organized through a single general elite; through diverse, competing intermediaries; or through direct participation by virtually the whole population in all levels of cultural integration.[164] Each of these models seems to have existed in succession in the nineteenth century, and each carries different implications for defining the experience of community.

Before the American Revolution, as we have already noted, only a small proportion of the population was involved in extralocal political affairs. The mass of the population entered the political system through the local community or, more precisely, through their local community leaders who held a diffuse high status.[165] Although the social mobilization associated with the revolutionary experience opened the way for new patterns of socialization and political be-

162. See, for example, Richards, *Gentlemen of Property and Standing*.

163. The most notable of these is Arthur Vidich and Joseph Bensman, *Small Town in Mass Society* (Princeton University, 1968). See also Maurice Stein, *The Eclipse of Community* (New York: Harper, 1964); Roland L. Warren, *The Community in America* (Chicago: Rand McNally, 1963); and Daniel Elazar, *Cities of the Prairie* (New York: Basic, 1970).

164. See Sydel Silverman, "The Community–Nation Mediator in Traditional Central Italy," in *Peasant Society*, ed. Jack M. Potter et al. (Boston: Little, Brown, 1967), pp. 279–293.

165. This seems to be common in premodern societies. See F. X. Sutton, "Representation and the Nature of Political Systems," *CSSH*, 2 (1959), 1–10. For the United States, see Charles Sydnor, *American Revolutionaries in the Making* (New York: Macmillan [Collier], 1962).

havior, the political culture in the age of Jefferson remained essentially community oriented and elite dominated. Party appeals went to local elites who were expected to influence local voters.[166] This pattern of politics depended upon a notion that what held members of a local community together was more important than what divided them.

Economic developments eventually forced a reconsideration of this assumption. The growth of a market economy involving increasing numbers of ordinary Americans; the advent of periodic economic fluctuations, beginning with the panic of 1819; and conflict over fiscal and banking policies all made Americans, even in *socially integrated towns*, aware of a multiplicity of *economic interests*. This opened the way for competing political elites within local communities.[167] With ordinary citizens increasingly involved in economic activities that were formerly thought to be strictly in the province of the elite, a broader electorate was concerned with the effects and possibilities of state and even national economic legislation. Whereas political selection had earlier been honorific, citizens now tendered their vote in exchange for specific promises on policy issues. They were no longer willing to give a broad mandate to an acknowledged local elite who would then be free to do what they thought best for the whole community.[168]

This pattern of interest-group division and competing elites was dominant in the 1820s, and it represented something new in community affairs. Whatever it portended for the future, however, it did not, in the 1820s, change the local character of politics. Political orientations remained rooted in local life, even if the practice of politics sometimes highlighted divisions within a town. Only later, in the 1830s and 1840s, did the spirit of party and its institutional reality seem to make political divisions on the local level more im-

166. See Carl E. Prince, *New Jersey's Jeffersonian Republicans* (Chapel Hill: University of North Carolina, 1967), and Ronald Formisano, "Deferential-Participant Politics: The Early Republic's Political Culture, 1789–1840," *APSR*, 68 (1974): 476.

167. See George Dangerfield, *The Awakening of American Nationalism*, 1815–1828 (New York: Harper, 1965).

168. On this narrowing of authority granted to general elites in economic affairs, see Bender, "Law, Economy, and Social Values in Jacksonian America."

portant than social unity.[169] But even though community seems to have been breaking down in the political realm before the Civil War, there is evidence that the face-to-face patterns of social life in midwestern small towns continued to produce stable dominant parties in the late nineteenth century.[170]

The advent of mass political parties, developed first by the Jacksonian Democrats and then by the Whigs and Republicans, had important consequences for local life. Whereas the Whigs held firm to the older notion that political leadership was properly embedded in the organic pattern of social relations in the towns, the Jacksonians and—since innovation makes strange bedfellows—the antislavery groups experimented with new forms of political organization. These organizational patterns were made possible by innovations in communications technology that communicated directly from the center to the generality of Americans in their local communities. Power and status within this emerging political culture derived from position in the translocal organization rather than from local social standing.[171]

The impact on local life of this change in the structure and organization of national political power has yet to be fully explored by historians. The implications for individuals and communities seem, on the face of it, enormous. Wrenching Americans out of traditional and familiar relations to power could have been a trying experience, and indeed during the antebellum period there was a flowering of political pathologies, particularly fears of conspiracy. Americans and their local communities seem nonetheless to have weathered the change remarkably well. Perhaps the charismatic figure of Jackson eased the transition from the warm local political culture to the cold

169. See A. D. P. Van Buren, "Michigan in Her Pioneer Politics," *Historical Collections,* journal of the Michigan Pioneer Society, 17 (1892): 240–242.

170. See Melvyn Hammarberg, "Indiana Farmers and the Group Basis of the Late-Nineteenth Century Political Parties," *JAH*, 61 (1971): 114.

171. See Lynn L. Marshall, "The Strange Stillbirth of the Whig Party," *AHR*, 72 (1967): 445–468; Rogin, *Fathers and Children,* pp. 263, 267; Formisano, *Birth of Mass Political Parties,* p. 77; and Richard Hofstadter, *The Idea of a Party System* (Berkeley and Los Angeles: University of California, 1969); for antislavery organizations and local communities, see Richards, *Gentlemen of Property and Standing.*

bureaucratic one portended by the mass political parties. This spec-
ulation gains some weight by contrast with local reaction to organized antislavery. Here there was no sympathetic and warm
personality who could supply a myth with the power to mediate the
impact of external organization on the web of social life, and here
also was the complicating factor of racism. The result, as Leonard
Richards has demonstrated in his excellent study of antiabolition
mobs, was community division and personal violence.[172]

For all of the disorder and turmoil that characterized this era, one
is struck, however, by the essential political stability that ac-
companied this transformation in the culture of politcs. Any explanation must at this point be speculative, but perhaps it is to be
found in the persistence of locality-based community in the era of
emerging mass parties at the national level. Mass parties did not
replace local communities; instead they subtracted national politics
from the local social network in much the same way that the market
eventually subtracted economic affairs from the context of community. At the local level, as de Tocqueville recognized, politics
remained embedded in the "ordinary relations of life," while a
different order of "passions" was drawn out in the contest for political power in the larger society.[173]

Even when local politics were fought under the banners of the
national party, radically different political premises seem to have
been operative. Conflict was more intense and participation was
higher in national politics, but this did not signify the demise of
local politics. With national politics abstracted from local social relations, local politics returned to the quest for unity—and conformity—that had characterized the eighteenth century. While
national political rhetoric stressed division by class, by ethnic
group, and by ideological position, the impulse at the local level was
toward unification. In Stamford, Connecticut, for example, Estelle
Feinstein has discovered that for local elections "both mainstream

172. Ibid.
173. DeTocqueville, *Democracy in America,* 1:69–70.

parties made some attempt to represent the entire community and cut across ethnic and class lines."[174]

The most interesting point, however, is one that historians have not touched upon at all. If the national and local political cultures thrived in their parallel tracks, did they not sometimes impinge upon one another? Although anthropologists have devoted a great deal of energy to the problem of determining what the intrusion of a new party into an ongoing relationship means, historians have not yet explored this dimension of community life.[175] What happens to the pattern of class relations, for example, when an outside institution, whether it be the state or a national political party advocating the rights of the poor, enters the community? How are previous roles and expectations altered? These questions can be posed, but we have at present no answers for them.

◆

Until the 1820s, community problems were solved within multifunctional local institutions under the leadership of an unspecialized elite.[176] To the extent that the state government intruded into local affairs, it delegated responsibility to local communities to undertake some general purpose within the framework of local life. When local leaders perceived social problems, they thought in terms of local solutions. Educational leaders in the 1820s, for example, initially defined the task of reform in community terms. Only later, as Paul Mattingly explains, did they realize that they were facing a

174. Estelle F. Feinstein, *Stamford in the Gilded Age: The Political Life of a Connecticut Town, 1868–1893* (Stamford: Stamford Historical Society, 1973), pp. 34–43. This specific observation refers to the years immediately following the Civil War, but it seems to reflect mid-century behavior as well. See also Blumin, *Urban Threshold*, pp. 144, 148.

175. For a theoretical discussion on this point, see Owen Lynch, *The Politics of Untouchability* (New York: Columbia University, 1969), pp. 16–18, 202, 216. See also Vidich and Bensman, *Small Town in Mass Society*, and Richard Cloward and Frances Piven, *Regulating the Poor* (New York: Random House, Vintage, 1972).

176. This is typical of premodern societies; see Neil J. Smelser, "The Modernization of Social Relations," in *Modernization*, ed. Myron Weiner (New York: Basic, 1966), p. 118.

general social problem of state, regional, and even national dimensions.[177]

Even then, however, the community perspective remained fundamental. Although historians have recently made much of Horace Mann's role in advancing the cause of educational bureaucracies, his reform style was distinctive to the mid-nineteenth century. It would be a mistake to read twentieth-century patterns of institutional centralization into his notion of using moral suasion to persuade the state's communities, through their leaders, to adopt a common standard of education. Recall that his position as secretary of the board of education in Massachusetts gave him no coercive power, only the power to investigate and to write reports. In these reports, he articulated a refined model of education that he assumed was already embraced in a less precise way by all community leaders. Even in the realm of advocacy, the difference between his role and that characteristic of the twentieth-century bureaucratic reformer must be stressed. Mann's relation to local communities was not that of an outside expert, a specialized leader different in kind from local leaders. He was, instead, a general local leader writ large, and it was this that allowed him to move easily from educational reformer to Whig antislavery congressman, to western college president.[178]

After about 1870, a change is evident in schooling and school reformers. Educators became more professionalized, and the school shifted from being a reflection of the local community—slightly uplifted by Mann's rhetorical model—to being a local institution that served to connect local families to a wider world of impersonality and metropolitan organization. Even while acknowledging the reality of a fundamental change after the Civil War, it is necessary to insist that the local roots of American schools remained important

177. See Handlin and Handlin, *Commonwealth*, pp. 93–96, and Paul H. Mattingly, *The Classless Profession: American Schoolmen in the Nineteenth Century* (New York: New York University, 1975), chap. 1.

178. See Robert H. Wiebe, "The Social Functions of Public Education," *AQ*, 21 (1969): 149–151. For a discussion providing an example of his relations with local leaders, see Birdsall, *Berkshire County*, pp. 110–114.

through the end of the century and beyond. Although statewide organizations were intruding into local school affairs by 1870, local autonomy persisted. The educational uniformity identified with a mass society was not achieved in the nineteenth century; locality remained important.[179]

◆

Since the 1820s, Americans had become involved in more and more translocal activities—in national politics, in the economy, in religious and other voluntary associations—yet this was not strictly at the expense of local life. Although local communities became less exclusive as the context of social experience, if anything local life provided a stronger source of community identity.

The idea of the nation also grew stronger. If political horizons had earlier been limited to the local community or, at best, to the state, the formation of a national political culture extended them and complicated American politics. By the 1840s and 1850s, it was harder and harder for politicians to bridge local and national political cultures. National political integration began to restrict the politician's freedom to negotiate sectional interests, especially on the issue of slavery, over which competing versions of American ideology sought a national ratification that was achieved ultimately only through war.[180] Again, we have an enhancement of both local and national identities and interests, rather than the eclipse of one by the other. Indeed, during the Civil War itself, strong town identities led to "town bounty rivalries" as towns acted to fill their quotas for the sake of town pride and to protect local youth.[181]

179. See Wiebe, "The Social Function of Public Education," p. 156; Daniel Calhoun, *Intelligence of a People,* p. 67. See also Patricia A. Graham, *Community and Class in American Education, 1865–1918* (New York: Wiley, 1974).

180. Richard P. McCormick, "New Perspectives on Jacksonian Politics," *AHR,* 65 (1960): 288–301; idem., *The Second American Party System: Party Formation in the Jacksonian Era* (Chapel Hill: University of North Carolina, 1966); Frederick Jackson Turner, *The United States, 1830–1850* (New York: Norton, 1965); Joel H. Silbey, *The Shrine of Party: Congressional Voting Behavior, 1841–1852* (Pittsburgh: University of Pittsburgh, 1967); and Richard D. Brown, "Modernization and the Modern Personality in Early America, 1600–1865," *JIH,* 2 (1972): 224–225.

181. Eugene C. Murdock, *Patriotism Limited, 1862–1865* (Kent, Ohio: Kent State University Press, 1967), chap. 2, quotation from p. 27.

The town had proven remarkably resilient as the basis of community. There is evidence that, as the Civil War closed, local political and cultural life remained vital, and this provided the basis for a sense and experience of community. Even in economic affairs, there was a strong impulse toward community that nearly overcame the social divisions generated by the national market economy and by corporate capitalism in small but growing industrial towns. In Paterson, New Jersey, for example, as late as 1870, the workers remained integrated into a local community that was willing to protect them from exploitative "outside" corporations.[182] Life in America, it seems, was still oriented to the local community where, Robert Wiebe writes, "family and church, education and press, professions and government, all largely found their meaning by the way they fit one with another inside a town or a detached portion of a city."[183]

Community and the
Bifurcation of Society, 1850–1900

Although it is true that a locality-based pattern of community was apparent on a wide scale as late as 1870, it is perhaps more important to note the ways in which this community was changing. The bonds of sentiment and mutuality that defined community were now threaded through peoples' social experience in more complicated ways than they were a century earlier. Locality remained an important focus for community, but it no longer reigned supreme. Growth in the size and complexity of local life combined with important losses in local autonomy encouraged people to identify community with certain of its parts rather than with the whole, and for a few precocious individuals, social networks completely independent of territory defined a new kind of community.

182. See, for example, Feinstein, *Stamford in the Gilded Age*, pp. 134–135, 223, and the various essays, especially "Class, Status, and Community Power in Nineteenth Century Industrial Cities" by Herbert G. Gutman in his *Work, Culture, and Society in Industrializing America*.
183. Wiebe, *Search for Order*, p. 12.

The roots of this change extended far into the past, but by the third quarter of the nineteenth century, a cultural drama in which alternate patterns of community struggled to define themselves was being played out with the result that, about 1900, a new pattern of community clearly recognized as such by social commentators had emerged. This transformation in the character of community was associated with and was a product of a fundamental alteration in the structure of American society.

Brooks Adams observed in 1874 that "the whole history of the past ten years has been the legitimate result of the unresisted growth of the centralizing element." American political theories, he noted, were "now turning on ourselves and from a Federal Republic we are turning into a consolidated empire."[184] Changes in political ideas and practices are, however, only part of the story. The foundations of an older localized way of life were being eroded by new attitudes toward centralized authority and by innovations in transportation, communications, and organizational structure.

It is difficult to specify the timing of this challenge to the integrity of locality-based units of community life. The process was too complex, and it developed at different rates in different parts of the country. The earliest signs of change are noticeable as early as the 1830s in areas near large cities and with easy access to transportation. Some communities, on the other hand, remained isolated into the twentieth century.[185] By the 1870s, however, Americans were beginning to notice that towns were being drawn into the metropolitan orbit and that social institutions were being reshaped in ways that enhanced their translocal connections at the expense of their local ones.

Perhaps no contemporary articulated the nature and significance

---

184. Quoted in Geoffrey Blodgett, "A New Look at the Gilded Age: Politics in a Cultural Context," in *Victorian America,* ed. Daniel Walker Howe (Philadelphia: University of Pennsylvania, 1976), p. 106.

185. Marvin Meyers, *Jacksonian Persuasion,* pp. 235–236; Paul Cressy, "Social Disorganization and Reorganization in Harlan County, Kentucky," *ASR,* 14 (1949): 389–394; Charles P. Loomis and Olen Leonard, *Culture of a Contemporary Rural Community: El Cerrito, New Mexico* (Washington, D.C.: U.S. Department of Agriculture, 1941); Evon Z. Vogt and Ethel M. Albert, *People of Rimrock: A Study of Values in Five Cultures* (New York: Atheneum, 1970).

of this change with greater clarity than did Henry W. Bellows, a New York minister. In 1872 he wrote:

> Thousands of American towns, with an independent life of their own, isolated, trusting to themselves, in need of knowing and honoring native ability and skill in local affairs—each with its first-rate man of business, its able lawyer, its skilled physician, its honored representative, its truly *select-men*—have been pierced to the heart by the railroad which they helped to build to aggrandize their importance. It has gone through them in a double sense—stringing them like beads on a thread, to hang around the neck of some proud city. It has annihilated their old importance; broken up the dependence of their farmers upon the home traders; removed the necessity for any first-rate professional men in the village; . . . destroyed local business and taken out of town the enterprising young men, besides exciting the ambition of those once content with a local importance, to seek larger spheres of life.[186]

Institutions identified with the center gained in scope and influence, while local ones experienced a reduction. The distinction between communal ways and metropolitan ones was progressively sharpened, and social experience became bifurcated into what Tönnies called *Gemeinschaft* and *Gesellschaft*.

What actually happened to community during the Gilded Age and the Progressive era? It would not be quite correct to say that it broke down, but it did take on a radically new form and meaning. It was no longer easily identified with a geographic referent, particularly as a territorial whole. After 1870 or so, the communal experience could best be defined in terms of the *kind* of social relationship that had once characterized local life but which was no longer necessarily territorially based. Neither gemeinschaft nor gesellschaft is properly identified with a place; they are two radically different kinds of social relationship that can share the same territory. Although the city, for example, is often used as a symbol of gesellschaft, it is in fact the locus of both gemeinschaft and gesellschaft relationships.

The advent of gesellschaft during the nineteenth century might be described as an addition of gesellschaft to traditional gemeinschaft patterns of life. In a sense, such an interpretation is correct,

186. Henry W. Bellows, "The Townward Tendency," *The City*, 1872, p. 38.

for a new layer of social experience was indeed fastened onto the lives of Americans living in 1876 that did not exist in 1776. Yet there is an equally important sense in which the process was subtractive. Gesellschaft was created from materials, particularly in the economic and political realms, that were once a part of gemeinschaft and which were now removed from that social context and given an independent existence. Put differently, important economic and political elements of social life were torn from their communal context, reformed into segments of life with their own justification—that is, justification independent of community—and then added to a somewhat reduced gemeinschaft, producing an alternative and distinct realm of social experience.

Not only does the market offer the best symbol of the rational and calculating behavior characteristic of gesellschaft, but the actual historical development of the market, its institutions, and its psychology constitutes a crucial element in the emergence of a bifurcated society described in Tönnies's notion of *Gemeinschaft* and *Gesellschaft*. Although there was an extraordinary expansion in the scope and influence of the market during the nineteenth century, more than a quantitative increase in market activities is involved; there was a qualitative change in the nature and role of the market during the first century of American nationhood.

The market economy, Karl Polanyi has argued in his compelling book *The Great Transformation*, did not become a central social fact in even the most economically advanced western nations until the nineteenth century. He points out that a people involved in trade are not necessarily involved in a market economy. In a trading economy, economic activities are "embedded in social relations." In a market economy, however, economic activities are taken out of this social context and become an autonomous system of relationships. "Once the economic system is organized in separate institutions, based on specific motives and conferring special status," Polanyi writes, "society must be shaped in such a manner as to allow that system to function according to its own laws."[187] Whether this

187. Karl Polanyi, *The Great Transformation* (New York: Farrar & Rinehart, 1944), pp. 43, 57. See also George Dalton, ed., *Primitive, Archaic, and Modern*

split necessarily implies market dominance in society might usefully be debated and put to the empirical test, but Polanyi's statement does seem to describe an essential aspect of the change from the socially embedded economic activity characteristic of the colonial period toward what we recognize as the modern American economy.

Trade in colonial America was firmly rooted in a social and cultural context. It was bounded by networks of personal relationships and by religious, political, and social ideas and customs. The public lives of merchants and traders were confined by a many-dimensioned social web. Merchants were not narrowly economic either in the way they preceived themselves as merchants or in the way they were preceived by others. Economic activity alone did not yet confer status, nor were exclusively economic goals legitimate.[188]

During the nineteenth century, this pattern was gradually altered, but one must not exaggerate the rate of change. As late as mid century, New York merchants acted out social roles rather than narrowly economic ones, and they sought to perpetuate this orientation in the socialization of young men entering the mercantile profession. Not until 1870, according to Clarence Danhof, did American farmers unambiguously orient their production to the market.[189]

Economies: Essays of Karl Polanyi (Garden City, N.Y.: Doubleday, 1968); Eric Wolf, "The Spanish in Mexico and Central America," in *Economic Development and Social Change*, ed. George Dalton (Garden City, N.Y.: Natural History Press, 1971), pp. 228–256; Redfield, *Peasant Society and Culture;* R. H. Tawney, *Religion and the Rise of Capitalism* (New York: New American Library, Mentor, 1926); and David Harvey, *Social Justice and the City* (Baltimore: Johns Hopkins, 1973), p. 282.

188. For the complexity of the merchant's social role, see Bailyn, *New England Merchants in the Seventeenth Century;* Frederick B. Tolles, *Meeting House and Counting House: The Quaker Merchants of Colonial Philadelphia* (New York: Norton, 1963); Arthur H. Cole, "The Tempo of Mercantile Life in Colonial America," *Business History Review*, 33 (1959): 277–299; J. E. Crowley, *This Sheba Self: The Conceptualization of Economic Life in Eighteenth Century America* (Baltimore: Johns Hopkins, 1974). For evidence of the lack of legitimacy for narrowly economic activity in the early nineteenth century, see Fred Somkin, *Unquiet Eagle: Memory and Desire in the Idea of American Freedom, 1815–1860* (Ithaca, N.Y.: Cornell University, 1967), esp. chap. 1.

189. See Allan S. Horlick, *Country Boys and Merchant Princes: The Social Control of Young Men in New York* (Lewisburg, Pa.: Bucknell University, 1975); Clarence

The distinction between premodern and modern American economic activity needs to be phrased with some precision. Americans at the outset of the nineteenth century did not lack rationality, a concern for efficiency, or a willingness to work hard in behalf of their self-interest. What they lacked, from a modern perspective, was an autonomous economic institution legitimizing and facilitating the pursuit of economic goals outside of the web of social networks and cultural traditions.[190] This was the market. Different cultural groups within American society made the shift from the so-called premodern moral economy to a modern market orientation at different rates. Although some groups may to this day retain a certain allegiance to the traditional economic notions, after 1870, large and important groups in America had made the shift.[191]

The market was primary in the transformation that separated the late eighteenth century from the late nineteenth century. If the founding fathers assumed that trade, which they favored, would remain tightly controlled by the traditional moral and social sanctions in local communities, the Constitution they wrote allowed for the development of an autonomous market.[192] The abstract and translocal market increasingly challenged the family and community as a foundation for social order.[193] Market and community

---

Danhof, *Change in Agriculture: The Northern United States, 1820–1870* (Cambridge: Harvard University, 1969). Even after this date, as Richard Hofstadter has pointed out, the noneconomic rhetoric of the family farm and agrarian virtue persisted. See his *Age of Reform* (New York: Random House, Vintage, 1955).

190. For this conceptual distinction, see Manning Nash, *Primitive and Peasant Economic Systems* (San Francisco: Chandler, 1966), pp. 66–67.

191. For some suggestion of the conflicts inherent between moral and economic imperatives in the organization of work, see Gutman, *Work, Culture, and Society,* chap. 1. Different groups in the population responded in terms of their own cultural tradition, and this may account in part for the differential "success" reported in social mobility studies. See Thernstrom, *Other Bostonians,* and James Henretta, "The Quantification of Consciousness" (Paper delivered at The Conference on Quantification in Early American History, Stony Brook, N.Y., June, 1975).

192. On the importance of the Constitution for the development of a market economy, see Hurst, *Law and the Conditions of Freedom,* pp. 44–48, and Bruchey, *Roots of American Economic Growth,* pp. 96–98.

193. Rogin, *Fathers and Children,* pp. 31–36.

became alternative and competing patterns of order. Social experience, as a result, was bifurcated. At the core of this division, especially after the Civil War, was the conflict between community and the market, gemeinschaft and gesellschaft, as kinds of social interaction.[194]

Although the market was central to the emergence of gesellschaft and provides the most effective symbolic representation of its social meaning, the bifurcation of society can be stated in alternative terms. During the course of the nineteenth century, the distinction between public and private activities, or spheres of life, was sharpened. Public activities were increasingly undertaken in the same spirit as market activity; notions of rationality, individual interest, functionalism, and impersonality were equally characteristic of the market and of public activity generally in the developing bifurcated society.[195] What had been a seamless web of community life broke into segments. Work, once securely planted in the context of family and locality, became separated from its traditional social context. Whereas work, family, and town once supplied mutually reenforcing personal orientations, they became crosscutting sources of identity in the bifurcated society that emerged in the late nineteenth century.

The history of the family also illustrates the process of change. In the seventeenth century, as Philippe Ariés has shown for Europe and as Edmund S. Morgan and John Demos have shown for America, the wall between the family and the town was highly permeable.[196] With the rise of the market during the nineteenth

194. Michael J. Cassity, "Defending a Way of Life: The Development of Industrial Market Society and the Transformation of Social Relationships in Sedalia, Missouri, 1850–1890" (Ph.D. diss., University of Missouri, 1973).

195. See Hans Paul Bahrdt, "Public Activity and Private Activity as Basic Forms of City Association," in *Perspectives on the American Community*, ed. Roland L. Warren (Chicago: Rand McNally, 1966), pp. 78–85.

196. Philippe Ariés, *Centuries of Childhood: A Social History of Family Life* (New York: Random House, Vintage, 1962); Edmund S. Morgan, *The Puritan Family*, new ed. (New York: Harper, 1966); John Demos, *A Little Commonwealth: Family Life in Plymouth Colony* (New York: Oxford University Press, 1970), and idem., "The American Family in Past Time," *American Scholar*, 43 (1974): 422–446.

century, however, family life became more private. The competition and impersonality of public life enhanced the value of warmth and intimacy in family life.[197] The family became, in the words of Kirk Jeffrey, a "utopian retreat" where social relations were radically different from the impersonal and frightening world of gesellschaft.[198]

Concern over the specter of a bifurcated society lay at the root of many of nineteenth-century America's utopian programs. Within the labor movement, the Knights of Labor, founded in 1878, provides the most important example. The organizational structure of the Knights reflected a concern for traditional notions of community. The organization's basic unit, the district assembly, included all working people in a given locality with the exception of bankers, lawyers, and a few other nonproducers. With this stress upon community as opposed to craft solidarity, the movement sought to return work to a local communal context. The contrast between the Knights of Labor and the American Federation of Labor is striking on this point. The latter accepted the market and made a point of separating its economic goals from any moral, political, or social context.[199]

Even more interesting responses may be found in the utopian communities established from the 1840s onward. Although many were the product of a millenial religious impulse largely unchanged since the Middle Ages, others, including the most well-known ones,

197. See Clifford E. Clark, Jr., "Domestic Architecture as an Index to Social History: The Romantic Revival and the Cult of Domesticity in America, 1840–1870," *JIH*, 7 (1976): 33–56; Howard Gadlin, "Private Lives and Public Order: A Critical View of the History of Intimate Relations in the U.S.," *Massachusetts Review*, 17 (1976): 304–330; Katz, *People of Hamilton*, p. 206; Richard Sennett, *Families against the City: Middle Class Homes of Industrial Chicago, 1872–1890* (Cambridge: Harvard University, 1970).

198. Kirk Jeffrey, "The Family as Utopian Retreat from the City: The Nineteenth Century Contribution," *Soundings*, 55 (1972): 21–40. See also Christopher Lasch, "The Family as a Haven in a Heartless World," *Salmagundi*, no. 35 (1976), pp. 42–55.

199. See Charles P. LeWarne, "Labor and Communitarianism, 1880–1900," *Labor History*, 16 (1975): 393–407, and Gerald N. Grob, *Workers and Utopia: A Study of Ideological Conflict in the American Labor Movement, 1865–1900* (Evanston, Ill.: Northwestern University, 1961).

addressed themselves specifically to the impersonality, competition, and fragmentation that characterized the larger society. Albert Brisbane, the American spokesman for Fourier, continually railed against the false principles of association that characterized American economic life.[200] These reformers were disturbed by the disjunction between family or communal ways and societal ones. The preamble to the Articles of Agreement and Association at Brook Farm, for example, announced the intention "to substitute a system of brotherly cooperation for one of selfish competition." John Humphrey Noyes, founder of the Oneida Community, which was one of the most successful of all nineteenth-century intentional communities, declared his hope of extending the sincerity of the "family union beyond the little man-wife circle to large corporations."[201]

Noyes, who had experienced a personal crisis in New York City shortly before establishing his community, understood the impersonality and competition that characterized the emerging urban society,[202] yet he also believed that gemeinschaft need not retreat all the way into the isolated Victorian family. It could comprehend, he thought, a good portion of the ordinary life of men and women, encompassing what in most American towns was becoming differentiated into distinct public and private realms. Work, worship, recreation, and, in a complicated way, sex remained for Noyes properly embedded in the context of community. In his ideal image of modern society, one finds a series of tightly bounded gemeinschaft units in which most ordinary activities were undertaken in an environment of primary relationships. Interaction with the larger society, the world of gesellschaft, would be as a member of a fairly extensive community, rather than as an individual.

Only a few Americans, however, experienced the gemeinschaft envisioned by Noyes. For most Americans in the second half of the nineteenth century, a different and exceedingly complex pattern of

200. See, for example, Albert Brisbane, "False and True Association Contrasted," *The Harbinger,* 3 (November 17, 1846): 365–368.

201. William A. Hinds, *American Communities and Co-operative Colonies* (Chicago: C. H. Kerr, 1908), p. 252; John Humphrey Noyes, *History of American Socialisms* (Atlantic Highlands, N.J.: Hillary House, 1961), p. 23.

202. On Noyes in New York City, see Maren Lockwood Carden, *Oneida* (Baltimore: Johns Hopkins, 1969), pp. 27–29.

gemeinschaft and gesellschaft—one not yet charted by historians— defined their roles, statuses, and personal identities. The clear boundaries that had earlier marked the shape of community became diffuse and often distressingly difficult to specify. Americans, especially those in urbanizing areas, experienced a serious split in their social experience between communal ways of relating to people and the impersonal relations characteristic of gesellschaft.[203] One's role as a member of a family or a circle of friends became sharply differentiated from one's role and behavior in economic relations, in dealing with the government, or in relations with any large-scale organizations. Within the first sphere, communal patterns of behavior, with their emphasis on face-to-face relationships, affective bonds, and diffuseness of obligation, remained appropriate and functional, but people painfully learned that these communal ways did not work in the larger society where their public activities were undertaken.[204]

◆

Although it is common to speak of Americans as national citizens in the twentieth century, because they are involved with social organizations of national scale and with status referents in a national system of stratification, it is clear that distinctive patterns of culture, whether based upon class, ethnicity, religion, local tradition, or family heritage, affect the way in which particular individuals or groups relate and have related to national institutions.[205] These

203. For a brilliant evocation of this transformation in the social psychology of community life, see Georg Simmel, "The Metropolis and Mental Life," reprinted in *The Sociology of Georg Simmel*, ed. Kurt H. Wolff (New York: Free Press, 1950), pp. 409–424. For the progressive disjunction of familial and urban ways in nineteenth-century America, see Kirk Jeffrey, "Family History: The Middle-Class American Family in the Urban Context, 1830–1870" (Ph.D. diss., Stanford, 1972); idem., "Family as Utopian Retreat from the City"; Clark, "Domestic Architecture as an Index to Social History"; Gadlin, "Private Lives and Public Order"; Katz, *People of Hamilton;* Sennett, *Families against the City;* and Lasch, "Family as a Haven in a Heartless World."

204. Wiebe, *Search for Order*, p. 12.

205. On the notion of national citizenship, see Brian J. L. Berry, *The Human Consequences of Urbanisation* (New York: St. Martin's, 1973), p. 57, but for the necessary qualifications, see Steward, *Theory of Culture Change,* r. 50.

complexities were even more apparent in the second half of the nineteenth century.

By focusing on the shift from community to society, from personal to impersonal forms of social organization, historians have largely overlooked these complexities. What needs to be explored is the interplay of various kinds of statuses and orientations over time in a bifurcated society. Individuals were involved in different kinds of social relationships and held different statuses depending upon whether they were acting out a role as a member of a family, as political men and women, as followers of religious persuasions, or as participants in the economy. These roles were once mutually reenforcing and collectively constituted a community. By 1870, however, they were differentiated and often conflicting. In time, indeed, each developed its own autonomous conceptual framework within which social actions were framed. Some represented community, while others did not.

The interworkings of these dimensions of life in the past await investigation. While the sociologist Bernard Barber has attempted to distinguish analytically the multiple status systems that shape our lives, today historians have not pursued this sort of inquiry.[206] What characteristics bring high status within familial or communal contexts? In national institutions? How does success or a high level of commitment on one of these dimensions of social experience affect others? Does success on the gemeinschaft scale of values affect the possibilities of success in gesellschaft? For instance, have strong familial or communal commitments hampered the effective participation of some groups in the larger structures of the economy?[207]

These divisions between gemeinschaft and gesellschaft became a defining characteristic of American social life at the end of the nineteenth century. Americans found themselves in complicated pat-

---

206. Barber, "Family Status, Local-Community Status, and Social Stratification."
207. For evidence of positive empirical findings on this for contemporary America, see Gerhard Lenski, *The Religious Factor: A Sociological Study of Religion's Impact on Politics, Economics, and Family Life*, rev. ed. (Garden City, N.Y.: Doubleday, Anchor, 1963), p. 123.

terns of psychological and sometimes even physical mobility between these two worlds of social behavior. Even in small towns, life became segmented, with major divisions following fault lines introduced by the intrusion of translocal institutions and role identities. Social units smaller than the town were importantly involved with the metropolitan bureaucracy, and this transformed units of life, which now interacted with larger and bureaucratic ones. Diverse units of communal relations now had to establish viable patterns of interaction with uniform metropolitan bureaucracies.[208]

———◆———

To get at the changing meaning of community in the second half of the nineteenth century, historians must focus on tension and interaction rather than upon collapse. Although the equilibrium between community and society shifted, community never disappeared. It was, however, transformed.

The repeated pleas of Samuel P. Hays for a more systematic consideration of changes in the social structure seem to offer fruitful guideposts for the sort of work that needs to be undertaken. Historians, he writes, should study the "changing relationship between tendencies toward centralization and countertendencies toward decentralization; for example, in the cities between centralization focused on corporate systems, government, the central city, redevelopment, professionalization and higher education on the one hand and the decentralization of life in residential institutions— home, family, church, recreation, school, and suburbanization—on the other."[209]

Actually, the complexity is even greater than Hays allows, if one uses gemeinschaft and gesellschaft, instead of centralization and decentralization, as analytic dichotomies. Gemeinschaft and gesell-

208. For examples of this interaction drawn from the history of education, see Tyack, *One Best System*, pts. I and II, and Diane Ravitch, *The Great School Wars: New York City, 1805–1973* (New York: Basic, 1974).
209. Hays, "A Systematic Social History," p. 338. He has offered different versions of this statement in "Changing Political Structure of the City in Industrial America," pp. 7–8, and in "Development of Pittsburgh as a Social Order."

schaft patterns of social relations cross his dividing lines in very complicated ways. One might ask, for example, what significance community has within corporate and other occupational settings? Alternately, what is the role and significance of bureaucracy in the church? Each of these social units, and others, can be probed for different and changing patterns of gemeinschaft and gesellschaft.[210]

Social relations in these social units must be examined with great care because all is not always what it first appears to be. Only close attention to detail and context can reveal the actual cultural meanings in social interactions. Personalized relations in various economic structures might serve as an illustration. They do not always serve a communal or moral order; they may in fact serve a technical order. Patterns of personal relations that superficially seem to be communal may in fact serve the extrinsic goal of mobilizing capital and labor.[211] On the other hand, external forces, including metropolitan markets and governmental bureaucracies, can actually revitalize a traditional local moral order.[212]

Without a historical account of long-term changes in community, historians will be unable to explore the complexity of social interaction within the American social system. Although the preceding account has been highly, even rashly, speculative, it is historically grounded within the limits of space and of the existing historical literature. As such, I hope, it can serve as a narrative structure for the empirical studies we need. More immediately, it can serve as a framework for the investigation of social networks in the following chapter.

210. For communal and familial aspects of work, see, for example, Virginia Yans McLaughlin, "Like the Fingers of the Hand: The Family and Community Life of First-Generation Italian-Americans in Buffalo, New York, 1880–1930." (Ph.D. diss., SUNY-Buffalo, 1970), pp. 300–357; Neil J. Smelser, *Social Change in the Industrial Revolution* (Chicago: University of Chicago, 1959), pp. 180–312. For bureaucratic tendencies in the church, see Calhoun, *Professional Lives,* chap. 4.

211. See Wolf, "Spanish in Mexico and Central America," p. 240.

212. See, for example, Emilio Willems, "Peasantry and City: Cultural Persistence and Change in Historical Perspective: A European Case," *AA,* 72 (1970): 534; Loomis and Leonard, *Culture of a Contemporary Rural Community;* Conzen, *Frontier Farming in an Urban Shadow,* p. 150; and Kai T. Erikson, *Everything in Its Path: Destruction of Community in the Buffalo Creek Flood* (New York: Simon & Schuster, 1976), pp. 127–132.

Chapter Four

Social Networks and the Experience of Community

In contrast to the broad overview of the changing configuration of community in American history, I now seek an interior view. Here, the focus is on the individual and his or her social contacts, rather than on the container of social life. Georg Simmel suggested this sociological point of view in "The Metropolis and Mental Life," published in 1903. In this essay, perhaps the most evocative and stimulating consideration of the culture of cities ever written, Simmel insisted that "an inquiry into the inner meaning of specifically modern life . . . must seek to solve the equation which structures like the metropolis set up between the individual and superindividual contents of life."[1] From this vantage, it is possible to cast an eye over the range of social contacts that are available to an individual in different historical periods and judge which, if any, represent manifestations of community.

The problem of locating community in people's lives requires openness and sensitivity to the texture of social experience. Within the periodization and structure of community–society relationships already sketched out, it is possible now to turn to the perspective of the individual and ask with what kind of social units he or she has

1. Georg Simmel, "The Metropolis and Mental Life," in *The Sociology of Georg Simmel*, ed. Kurt H. Wolff (New York: Free Press, 1950), p. 409.

contact. What is the nature of each social aggregate? What is the character of social relations in each? Are they communal in quality? Does any particular group represent the experience of community for the individual? The rather open-ended strategy that this approach implies defeats most motives for false interpretation. In the process of mapping the social network, both positive and negative answers will, in their own ways, advance the investigation.

Locating Social Networks

What I am suggesting is a study of the network of social relations in which the individual is embedded. An important example of this sort of analysis is provided by the work of social anthropologists, mostly British, who found Wirth's theory inadequate in their studies of African urbanization. Men and women in African cities, they discovered, remained within the bonds of community, yet their communities were not simply locality based; they were founded upon very complex patterns of social interaction. In order to explain what they found, social anthropologists turned their attention to mapping the network of social relations and assessing the quality of particular relationships. "The network approach," according to J. Clyde Mitchell, "deliberately seeks to examine the way in which people may relate to one another in terms of several different normative frameworks at one and the same time and how a person's behaviour might in part be understood in light of the pattern of coincidence of these frameworks."[2]

This mode of apprehending the structure of social experience can accommodate a wide variety of data without prejudice. If social relations in a local area are not communal in quality, so be it. If a relationship between two physically separated individuals has the qualities of mutuality and sentiment associated with community, then such is the relationship. Some of these networks to

2. J. Clyde Mitchell, "The Concept and Use of Social Networks," in *Social Networks in Urban Situations: Analyses of Personal Relationships in Central African Towns,* ed. J. Clyde Mitchell (Manchester, England: Manchester University, 1969), p. 49.

which individuals are attached are partially inherited (e.g., the family); others are wholly constructed. Either way, they must be defined in each instance as either communal or noncommunal.[3]

The most important point about the network approach is its sensitivity to the particularity of the context. It leaves open the question of whether a specific social aggregate is a community or not. It is an empirical question to determine whether a neighborhood is a community or how far community penetrates a kin network. Indeed, it is so open that it can accommodate the discovery of several communal networks in the life of a particular individual—or none at all. The network approach has the great value, in other words, of making the researcher sensitive to the social ties available to the urbanite without restricting the interpretation of what is found.

The network approach has one final asset as a guide for research into the dimensions of community. It allows the researcher to probe incidences of convergence among various networks as well as incidences of divergence or conflict. Does the family network—and the ideals and expectations assimilated into it—conflict with the occupational network? Do people experience the various institutions in their society as converging forces or as segments pulling them in contradictory directions? The social network approach, it seems to me, offers the possibility of locating the dimensions of community in people's lives and of probing the interplay of these communal orientations with the larger society.[4]

Can an anthropological approach to the texture of social life based upon a method of observation not available to the historian be adapted to the limitations of historical evidence? I suspect that it

3. Although it is beyond the scope of my present purposes, one might also attempt to discriminate among the various noncommunal networks.

4. For an introduction to network theory, see Mitchell, "Concept and Use of Social Networks"; A. L. Epstein, "Urbanization and Social Change in Africa," in *The City in Newly Developing Countries*, ed. Gerald Breese (Englewood Cliffs, N.J.: Prentice-Hall, 1969), pp. 246–284; Claude S. Fischer, "The Study of Urban Community and Personality," in *Annual Review of Sociology*, ed. Alex Inkeles (1975), pp. 67–89; Paul Craven and Barry Wellman, "The Network City," *Sociological Inquiry*, 43 (1973): 57–88; and J. A. Barnes, "Networks and Political Process," in *Social Networks in Urban Situations*, ed. Mitchell, pp. 51–76.

can, but social historians will have to go beyond the census tract in order to do it. They will have to study novels, autobiographies, correspondence, diaries, and biographies along with the information they derive from quantitative analysis of census manuscripts. Some of the possibilities inherent in this approach to historical materials are evident in Alan MacFarlane's *Family Life of Ralph Josselin,* a study of a seventeenth-century English clergyman.[5] MacFarlane, who was trained as an anthropologist, reconstructed Josselin's network of social relations from his diary. With whom did he have contact? What was the nature of these relationships? How did relationships with kin differ from those with friends? Nuclear family from more distant kin? Friends from neighbors? In this way, MacFarlane got at the structure and quality of Josselin's social relationships.

Much the same can be done with American diaries. George Templeton Strong, perhaps nineteenth-century New York's most notable diarist, provides an example.[6] This diary, covering the years from the 1830s to the 1870s, reveals a rich texture of community at the core of Strong's social life amidst the flux and change of the American metropolis. It is difficult to determine for certain the quality of every relationship that appears in the diary, but it is clear that he found the experience of community within a network of at least thirty people. The threads out of which this fabric of community was woven are diverse, but there are certain prominent figures in the design that give it order: family and kin, Trinity church, and Columbia College. His experience on the executive committee of the United States Sanitary Commission during the Civil War also nourished relationships that were part of his experience of community.

His immediate family (parents, wife, and children) was central to

5. Alan MacFarlane, *The Family Life of Ralph Josselin: A Seventeenth Century Clergyman* (Cambridge: At the University, 1970).

6. What follows is based upon a systematic analysis of Strong's diary done under my direction by Jeffrey K. Eichler, a graduate student at New York University. The diary has been published in a four-volume condensed and bowdlerized edition. See George Templeton Strong, *Diary,* ed. Allan Nevins and Milton Halsey Thomas (New York: Macmillan, 1952).

his life. He lived next door to his parents for much of his married life, and his relationship with his wife and her family was deep and loving. The community created by his kin, however, extended beyond his immediate family. He was deeply involved in an extensive kinship network, including men and women, that comprehended local and distant kin. Charley Strong, a third cousin, lived a block away, and Samuel B. Ruggles, his father-in-law, lived a five-minute walk away, but his relationship with his half-sister Eloise Lloyd Derby, who lived in Boston, was as intense, despite the distance, as his relationships with local kin, and it was maintained over the years through exchanges of visits.

Not all members of the extended family were within the bounds of Strong's community. Some were mere acquaintances; some never even appear in the diary. Others, however, had a uniquely intimate relationship with Strong. Two men stand out in this respect: James Ruggles and Samuel B. Ruggles. In the course of his frequent troubles with his second son and namesake, Strong often brought these men together into a "conseil de famille." (Interestingly, Strong's own father seems to have bolstered his paternal authority a generation earlier by bringing two close friends into the family circle.) Within Strong's household, it was even possible for a servant to be absorbed into the circle of familial intimacy, as in the case of Lizzie Conlon. When she left Strong's house to marry, he recorded his sadness at losing one of the family. However familial her relationship appeared in the household's daily experience, it was limited nonetheless. After she left Strong's house to return to the world of the working class as a wife, there are no more references to her in the diary.

Family, however, constituted only one dimension of Strong's experience of community. Bonds of mutuality and sentiment were established with schoolmates at Columbia, and he developed a close bond with at least one of his teachers. The communal bonds that linked him to his classmate George Anthon developed out of their common experience at Columbia and as law students in Strong's father's office. It was also in this office that a communal relationship was formed with Charley Strong, who became his legal partner and life-long companion. Charley's being a third cousin had not in itself made him a member of Strong's community. It is important to recognize that the vast majority of Strong's Columbia and professional associates never became a part of his community. Most of his professional relationships were segmental and instrumental. Some of them were more diffuse and mutual, but they were usually a community of limited liability. While ongoing, they had a certain affective quality and commitment, but changed circumstances or migration easily broke these bonds.

The experience of working together with men of his own social class at Columbia, Trinity, and the Sanitary Commission occasionally produced bonds of community, but not always. For example, Strong worked closely with John J. Astor as a Columbia trustee and Trinity vestryman, and although he liked Astor, a certain distance and uneasiness always marked their relationship. Other long-time associates never became more than casual acquaintances. Alexander Bradford provides an example. He and Strong knew each other for years. They were both members of the bar and served together at Columbia and Trinity, but they never came to know each other well, as Strong acknowledged when he learned, upon Bradford's death, that his associate had been an alcoholic. "How little we know of people we meet every day," Strong recorded in his diary. He knew and valued the intimate friendship of several other trustees, but the group as a whole, which he once called the "Board of Incurables," did not constitute a community for him. His relationships with the Columbia faculty were almost exclusively instrumental. Strong's relationships at Trinity reveal a similar range and diversity of responses. His work on the United States Sanitary Commission's executive committee resulted primarily in mere acquaintances, yet during the months and years he served there, an association with Horace Binney, Jr., ripened into a bond of community.

Institutions provided a context for many of Strong's experiences of community, and these relationships could therefore be complicated by instrumental concerns. Sometimes communal and instrumental impulses reenforced each other; at other times the opposite occurred. Two examples will suffice. The first pertains to the famous

Gibbs Affair at Columbia. Strong's intimate friend Wolcott Gibbs, one of the nation's leading scientists and a professor at the Free Academy of New York (later City College), was proposed for a professorship at Columbia. Strong and Ruggles strongly supported him, but the board rejected him because of his Unitarian religious beliefs. In supporting Gibbs, Strong was aiding a person with whom he felt a deep sense of community, yet in reading Strong's comments on the affair, it is clear that he supported Gibbs just as much because he was the best scholar available and because he felt that religious tests were inapppropriate in a true university. Indeed, Richard Hofstadter detects an anticipation of modern notions of academic freedom in Strong's statements on the case.[7]

If communal and instrumental orientations overlapped in the Gibbs case, Strong's relationship with Frederick Law Olmsted during their involvement with the U.S. Sanitary Commission provides a contrast. Strong developed a deep personal regard for Olmsted during the course of their work together, yet the structural environment within which this relationship developed brought the aspect of power into it. (Strong was a member of the executive committee, while Olmsted was the executive secretary.) When Olmsted seemed to be arrogating power that Strong felt belonged to the board, instrumental values became more salient than communal ones in their relationship, and Strong seems not to have regretted Olmsted's resignation and migration to California.

The association of community with important New York institutions suggests another of its dimensions: It can be tied to political and economic power. Although not everyone in Strong's class was in his community, everyone in his community was in his class. These communal ties were the basis of great institutional power at Columbia, Trinity, and in the Union League Club. The latter institution is particularly instructive in this respect. It was founded by members of Strong's class and community after the Civil War (partly as a result of their experience with the Sanitary Commis-

7. See Richard Hofstadter, *Academic Freedom in the Age of the College* (New York: Columbia University, 1955), pp. 269–274.

sion) in order to give organized force in the nation at large to their cultural and political ideals. This association of community with institutional power was not unique with Strong. It may, in fact, partially define an elite. By contrast, the communal bonds of the poor seldom run to centers of power and may even serve to isolate them further.

There are literally hundreds of diaries, representing people of all social classes, ethnic groups, regions, and kinds of settlement—rural, small town, and urban—that wait to be exploited in this fashion by historians. Correspondence offers much the same opportunity. Carroll Smith-Rosenberg has shown that it is possible to reconstruct the networks of community in the lives of nineteenth-century women from surviving correspondence, and Theodore Rosengarten's transcription of Nate Shaw's oral autobiography is an example of a marvellous source documenting the social networks that shaped the life of a nonliterate historical figure.[8]

Family, Community, and Society

Much more research—work that this essay will perhaps call into being—needs to be done before a comprehensive account of the various contexts of community in American history can be written, but because gemeinschaftlich relationships have been identified historically with the family, it is possible to use recent scholarship in family history to demonstrate the approach I am recommending. The changing character of this one aspect of community over time can be illustrated in the process. It is also possible with this approach to suggest some of the points of contact, conflict, and accommodation that have marked the relationships between gemeinschaft and gesellschaft at different periods and among different social groups. Moreover, as discussion of the family always raises the question of socialization, we may inquire what role is performed by the family, other institutions, or both in socializing

8. Carroll Smith-Rosenberg, "The Female World of Love and Ritual: Relations between Women in Nineteenth Century America, *Signs*, 1 (1975): 1–29; Theodore Rosengarten, *All God's Dangers: A Life of Nate Shaw* (New York: Knopf, 1974).

children into the two patterns of social experience that characterize a bifurcated society.

To pursue this theme adequately, it is essential to abandon the common notions, evident in the theories of Wirth and Parsons, with which we began, notions that assume either a unilinear weakening of the traditional family or a direct movement from extended to isolated nuclear family forms as a consequence of urbanization and modernization.[9] Historians and sociologists have recently exposed several flaws in these theories. The nuclear family seems to have antedated modern urban life, and there is a great deal of evidence documenting the fact of extensive kin networks forming a community in modern cities.[10] In some instances, the historical movement between family types even goes in the "wrong" direction during the course of urban development, from nuclear to extended family patterns. The movement may, in fact, be back and forth, and during the course of their life cycles, individuals might find themselves in different family forms.[11] Finally, the implicit assumption

9. See Louis Wirth, "Urbanism as a Way of Life," *AJS*, 44 (1938): 1–24; Talcott Parsons, "The Kinship System of the Contemporary United States," *AA*, 45 (1943): 22–38; and idem., "The Normal American Family," in *Man and Civilization: The Family's Search for Survival*, ed. Seymour Farber et al. (New York: McGraw-Hill, 1965), pp. 31–50.

10. The material on these issues is voluminous; for a discussion of the major current issues and a survey of the literature, see Bert N. Adams, "Isolation, Function, and Beyond: American Kinship in the 1960s," *Journal of Marriage and the Family*, 32 (1970): 575–597. See also Tamara K. Hareven, "Modernization and Family History: Perspectives on Social Change," *Signs*, 2 (1976): 190–206, and Peter Laslett, ed., *Household and Family in Past Time* (Cambridge: At the University, 1972).

11. Lutz K. Berkner, "The Stem Family and the Developmental Cycle of the Peasant Household: An Eighteenth-Century Austrian Example," *AHR*, 77 (1972): 398–418; Christopher Hill, *Society and Puritanism in Pre-Revolutionary England*, 2d ed. (New York: Schocken, 1967), chap. 14; Philippe Ariès, *Centuries of Childhood: A Social History of Family Life* (New York: Random House, Vintage, 1962), pp. 365–407; Philip J. Greven, Jr., *Four Generations: Population, Land, and Family in Colonial Andover, Massachusetts* (Ithaca, N.Y.: Cornell University, 1970); Lawrence Cremin, *American Education: The Colonial Experience* (New York: Harper, 1970), pp. 135, 519; David Herlihy, "Family Solidarity in Medieval Italian History," in *Economy, Society and Government in Medieval Italy*, ed. David Herlihy et al. (Kent: Kent State University, 1969), pp. 173–184; Diane Owen Hughes, "Urban Growth and Family Structure in Medieval Genoa," *Past and Present*, no. 66 (1975), pp. 3–28; Virginia Yans McLaughlin, "Like the Fingers of the Hand: The Family

in these theories—that the family is merely a passive, dependent variable in the historical process—has been challenged.[12] In other words, the community that forms around the family can be a dynamic element in interactions that define historical and contemporary social experience.

The interrelationships among the individual, the family, and the larger society are enormously complex. What we want to know here is how the family's place in the total organization of social life has changed and how this might affect its internal workings, including the formation of personal identity for children reared in it. All of this, of course, bears upon its quality as a community. To begin to capture these crucial dimensions of family life in the social networks that give meaning to people's lives, historians and sociologists will need to show sensitivity to the internal dynamics of the family, its boundaries, and its linkages with other social aggregates, such as circles of friends, neighbors, fellow workers, and political and economic institutions. It would be possible to begin an inquiry into the historical contexts of community with any one of these points on social networks in order to plot the configuration of community in people's lives. I am working from the perspective of the family because at present the evidence is richer and because I think the family is crucial for any discussion of community in American history.

In relations within the family and between the family and public life, what changes occurred between 1600 and 1900? Here we must consider the changing definitions and boundaries of the family over

and Community Life of First-Generation Italian-Americans in Buffalo, New York, 1880–1930" (Ph.D. diss., SUNY-Buffalo, 1970), p. 87; Marvin Sussman and Lee Burchinal, "Kin Family Network: Unheralded Structure in Current Conceptualizations of Family Functioning," *Marriage and Family Living*, 24 (1962): 235; Mark Hutter, "Transformation of Identity, Social Mobility and Kinship Solidarity," *Journal of the Marriage and the Family*, 32 (1970): 133–137.

12. Virginia Yans McLaughlin, "Like the Fingers of the Hand," pp. 428–431; idem., "Patterns of Work and Family Organization: Buffalo's Italians," *JIH*, 2 (1971): 299–314. See also Michael Anderson, *Family Structure in Nineteenth Century Lancashire* (Cambridge: At the University, 1971), and William J. Goode, *World Revolution and Family Values* (New York: Free Press, 1963), p. 15.

time. To what degree have family members distinguished the character of their mutual relationships from those with others? How has the family as an institution compared with other social institutions that make up an individual's social network? What is the nature of the interplay among these social units?

In the seventeenth century, family, town, and commonwealth were treated as larger and smaller versions of the same kind of social interaction. "A family," John Winthrop could say in 1637, "is a little commonwealth, and a commonwealth is a great family." Experience in the family prepared one for participation in the community and its institutions. The family and the town, observes historian John Demos, "formed part of the same moral equation."[13] In the twentieth century, the boundaries between the family and the larger social institutions are sharper, and the family has a special emotional quality and character that distinguishes it from public associations.[14]

The relation of the family to the town and its institutions in the seventeenth century is best described by the image of concentric spheres. The boundary separating these spheres was highly permeable; taken all together, they formed a community. Inasmuch as the distinction we know today between public life and the privacy of the family had not yet developed, social relations inside and outside of the family were not sharply differentiated. The web

13. Winthrop quoted in Darrett B. Rutman, *American Puritanism* (Philadelphia: Lippincott, 1970), p. 72; John Demos, *A Little Commonwealth: Family Life in Plymouth Colony* (New York: Oxford University Press, 1970), p. 186. See also the statement by William Gouge (1662) printed on the frontispiece of Demos's book.

14. See Talcott Parsons and Robert Bales, *Family, Socialization and Interaction Process* (New York: Free Press, 1953), esp. pp. 9–19; Edward Shorter, *The Making of the Modern Family* (New York: Basic, 1975); Ariés, *Centuries of Childhood;* Richard Sennett, *Families against the City: Middle Class Homes of Industrial Chicago, 1872–1890* (Cambridge: Harvard University, 1970); John Demos, "The American Family in Past Time," *American Scholar,* 43 (1974): 422–446. Cf. Christopher Lasch, "What the Doctor Ordered," *New York Review,* 22 (December 11, 1975): 50–54, and Richard Sennett, *The Fall of Public Man* (New York: Knopf, 1977), esp. pp. 177–178.

of community drew all important social networks together. In this context, it was easy and common for parents to place their teenage children to be reared in other families. Just as it was relatively easy to move outside of the family to the town, it was also easier for townspeople to intervene in the affairs of the family. New England town authorities, for example, might censure a husband and wife for being disrespectful of each other or for rearing their children badly. The rather vague family boundaries, however, seem to have contributed to the maintenance of rather firm boundaries at the level of the town.[15]

By 1900, towns were less cohesive, and the idea of family privacy had bolstered the boundaries of most American families against such official intrusion, but this development had important variations of two kinds, both associated with class. Throughout the nineteenth century and in our own time, social workers have been allowed to penetrate the boundaries of lower class families at will, and the families of many working-class and poor people tend in general to be less firmly bounded than middle-class families. Marc Fried, for example, argues that working-class groups typically extend a kinship orientation to relations with "local friends and neighbors."[16]

These few observations reveal that the question of who is in the family has no fixed answer. Particular historical and social circumstances produce different patterns of family life. It is impossible to rely entirely upon the simple distinction between nuclear and extended families. Over the course of American history, the communal relations conducted in a familial idiom have extended—in various combinations—to nuclear family groups, to resident kin, to resident nonkin, to nonresident kin, and to nonresident nonkin. In colonial America, for instance, the experience of community based upon family feelings included mother, father and children living in a

---

15. Edmund S. Morgan, *The Puritan Family*, new ed. (New York: Harper, 1966), esp. chap. 6. For a theoretical discussion of Puritan boundary maintenance, see Yehudi A. Cohen, "Social Boundary Systems," *Current Anthropology*, 10 (1969): 113.

16. Bernard Farber, *Guardians of Virtue: Salem Families in 1800* (New York: Basic, 1972), p. 200; Marc Fried, *The World of the Urban Working Class* (Cambridge: Harvard University, 1973), p. 226.

single household, but these ties also included servants, adult boarders, and other children living within the household, as well as kin,
friends, neighbors (often coterminous with the town), and also kin
who had moved to distant towns. Such geographic extensions of the
family, maintained by visits, correspondence, and today, telephone,
have always been a crucial aspect of its function as a community,
although there has been a long-term shift from patriarchal to more
egalitarian forms of extended-family cohesion.[17]

Colonial American families accepted nonkin into the household as
family members. Children placed in a nonparental home, for example, were not treated as outsiders, and adult boarders were not
considered intruders but members of the family. This pattern seems
to have continued into the nineteenth century. In the homes of
Hamilton, Ontario, during the 1850s, for example, there was "no
very clear distinction between relatives and boarders." With the
bifurcation of society, however, the otherness of nonfamily members was significantly enhanced. By the end of the nineteenth century, the dominant middle-class household was redefined. It became
more privatized, and the individuals it included were restricted to
the biological family—mother, father, children. Boarders and servants were now defined as strangers, and they were gradually excluded from the increasingly private sanctuary of the middle-class
home.[18]

This revolution in the definition of the family and household pro-

17. Linda A. Bissell, "Family, Friends, and Neighbors: Social Interaction in
Seventeenth Century Windsor, Connecticut" (Ph.D. diss., Brandeis, 1973); Greven,
Four Generations, p. 254. For the middle and southern colonies, see Randolph
S. Klein, *Portrait of an Early American Family: The Shippens of Pennsylvania
across Five Generations* (Philadelphia: University of Pennsylvania, 1975), p. 132,
and Darrett B. Rutman, "The Social Web: A Prospectus for the Study of the Early
American Community," in *Insights and Parallels*, ed. William L. O'Neill (Minneap-
olis: Burgess, 1973), pp. 57–123. The modern version of this phenomenon is discussed in Eugene Litwack, "Occupational Mobility and Extended Family Cohesion,"
ASR, 25 (1960): 10.

18. David H. Flaherty, *Privacy in Colonial New England* (Charlottesville: University of Virginia, 1972), pp. 66, 69; Michael B. Katz, *The People of Hamilton,
Canada West* (Cambridge: Harvard University, 1975), p. 232; and John Modell
and Tamara Hareven, "Urbanization and the Malleable Household: An Examination
of Boarding and Lodging in American Families," *Journal of Marriage and the
Family*, 35 (1973): 467–479.

vides the context for what has been written of the isolated nuclear family and, especially, of the isolated middle-class woman. Caution, however, is necessary here. This alteration of the home's boundaries did not sever relations with nonresident kin, whether they lived in the same neighborhood or in distant towns. The women in these families were not cut off from extensive kin networks; Carroll Smith-Rosenberg rightly observes that, for them, "emotional ties between nonresidential kin were deep and binding." Although these kin relations provided the closest and most prevalent communal ties outside of the home, nineteenth-century Americans often extended this network to include close primary relationships with friends as well as kin.[19] Nonetheless, the family as a form of social interaction had become sharply differentiated from a wide range of social experiences in people's lives that were not in any sense part of a community.

Change and the contraction of certain boundaries have marked the history of the dominant middle-class family, but there has been substantial continuity in poorer, black American families over the past century and a half—a continuity that may derive from their long-term economic and racial victimization. For this social group, the family has historically displayed broadly inclusive boundaries. Extensive slave communities, according to Herbert G. Gutman, were bound together by the "immediate family and the enlarged kin group." Southern slaves and, after the Civil War, freedmen augmented their families with what Gutman calls "fictive kin," non-related aunts and uncles who were treated as family members.[20]

A recent study of poor, black families in urban America by anthropologist Carol Stack suggests the continuing significance of this pattern of family and community life. The complexity and intermingling of familial and communal relations is reflected in her description of the structure and operation of the contemporary, poor, black family. This family, she writes, is "the smallest, orga-

19. Smith-Rosenberg, "The Female World of Love and Ritual," p. 11; Katz, *People of Hamilton,* pp. 107–108.

20. Herbert G. Gutman, *The Black Family in Slavery and Freedom, 1750–1925* (New York: Pantheon, 1976), pp. 216–229, 260. See also Crandall Shiffett, "The Household Composition of Rural Black Families: Louisa County Virginia, 1880," *JIH,* 6 (1975): 235–260.

nized, durable network of kin and nonkin who interact daily, providing for the domestic needs of children and assuring their survival. The family network is diffused over several kin-based households, and fluctuations in household composition do not significantly affect cooperative familial arrangements." Fictive aunts and uncles, even a "play daddy," are all part of the family, and an extensive range of "social relations are conducted with the idiom of kinship."[21]

The degree to which the family merges into a more extended network of gemeinschaft varies, not only over time, but also among class and cultural groups. This variation raises some interesting questions about the character of community and the internal workings of the family. Recent research on modern families and their social networks indicates that a deep involvement in an extrafamilial network of community encourages segregated roles for husbands and wives, whereas weaker involvements seem to produce more sharing activities.[22] Was this inverse relationship, which so complicates any understanding of the meaning and consequences of community, characteristic of earlier periods? Or were familial and extrafamilial forms of community mutually reenforcing? How has the bifurcation of society affected the definition of these two dimensions of communal experience?

In tracing the various extensions of community in an individual's life, one must be careful not to assume that certain social forms are always and obviously characterized by mutuality and sentiment. It is a mistake, for example, to expect every friendship in an individual's social network to represent a dimension of his or her community. Eric Wolf has pointed out that friendship can be expressive or instrumental in its primary orientation, and even the language of family, as Eugene Genovese has shown, can be linked to instrumen-

---

21. Carol B. Stack, *All Our Kin: Strategies for Survival in a Black Community* (New York: Harper, 1974), pp. 31, 58–60.

22. Elizabeth Bott, *Family and Social Network*, 2d ed. (London: Tavistock, 1971). Although she reviews American studies, her basic data is from England. For evidence from American cities supportive of her theory, see Marc Fried, *The World of the Urban Working Class* (Cambridge: Harvard University, 1973), p. 95; Gerald D. Suttles, *Social Order of the Slum* (Chicago: University of Chicago, 1968); and Herbert Gans, *The Urban Villagers* (New York: Free Press, 1962).

tal and exploitative social and economic relationships.[23] By contrast, work groups can constitute a community, and urban historians have shown that family ties constituted an essential aspect of the nineteenth-century business system.[24] It is the task of the historian and the sociologist to specify the circumstances under which these relationships are and are not a community.

Dual Socialization

With the advent of a bifurcated society that involved men and women simultaneously in gemeinschaft and gesellschaft, their social and psychological experiences were greatly complicated. They had to learn to live in two distinct worlds, each with its own rules and expectations. They were involved in small communities, including family and friends, and at the same time, they identified with larger and more abstract social units: profession, class, and citizenship. If the family (or other forms of community) retained a continuing significance, it is also true that the whole configuration of social experience—and with it, community—was transformed.

This social fact produced psychological conflicts that were noted by Charles Horton Cooley at the beginning of the twentieth century. "The modern world," he wrote, "makes distracting claims upon us. Shall we go with our family . . . or break away in pursuit of a larger humanitarian ideal? . . . Shall we follow the morals of our church or those of our profession?"[25] In particular cases, one pat-

---

23. Eric Wolf, "Kinship, Friendship, and Patron–Client Relations in Complex Societies," in *The Social Anthropology of Complex Societies,* ed. Michael Banton (London: Tavistock, 1966), p. 10; Eugene Genovese, *Roll, Jordan Roll: The World the Slaves Made* (New York: Pantheon, 1974).

24. Tamara K. Hareven, "The Laborers of Manchester, New Hampshire, 1912–1922: The Role of Family and Ethnicity in Adjustment to Industrial Life," *Labor History,* 16 (Spring, 1975): 249–265; Thomas Bender, *Toward an Urban Vision: Ideas and Institutions in Nineteenth-Century America* (Lexington: University of Kentucky, 1975), p. 31; Clyde Griffen and Sally Griffen, "Family and Business in a Small City: Poughkeepsie, New York, 1850–1880," *JUH,* 1 (1975): 316–338; Katz, *People of Hamilton,* p. 190. See also Elizabeth Pleck, "Two Worlds in One," *JSH,* 10 (1976): 178–195.

25. Charles H. Cooley, *Social Process* (New York: Scribner's, 1918), p. 253.

tern of social relations and ideals or the other was dominant, or salient, in shaping opinion and behavior.

The ability to respond appropriately to one or the other pattern of rules depended upon the development of a dual psychological repertoire. Americans found themselves possessed of two intertwined and simultaneously available repertoires. In the course of their lives, they had to recognize which one was called for in a particular instance.[26] When the "wrong" repertoire was chosen for a particular situation, unhappiness and frustration were inevitable. Some examples may clarify this point. Groups accustomed to "ordering their social relations along personal and familistic lines" typically had trouble when they came in contact with welfare bureaucracies or any other of "the formal institutions of American life."[27] The rather common American tendency to extend communal values appropriate only to face-to-face relationships to national politics has similarly produced frustration and, too often, what Richard Hofstadter has denoted a paranoid style in American politics. To reverse the example, those attempts to order familial relations on the basis of the rules appropriate to the larger political world, something associated with some contemporary versions of permissive parenthood that stress an essentially political equality of parents and children, seem rather predictably to lead to unhappiness and disappointment.[28]

Just how this psychological complexity is developed and how it works (or worked) is not entirely clear. Amos Hawley has observed that the individual is born into a small, homogeneous, and intimate group and then moves into a larger universe of impersonality and

---

26. On the notion of dual socialization, see Charles A. Valentine, "Deficit, Difference, and Bicultural Models of Afro-American Behavior," *HER*, 41 (1971), esp. pp. 141–142.

27. McLaughlin, "Like the Fingers of the Hand," p. 203.

28. See Peter Laslett, "The Face to Face Society," in *Philosophy, Politics and Society*, ed. Peter Laslett (Oxford: Blackwell, 1967), pp. 157–184; Richard Hofstadter, *The Paranoid Style in American Politics* (New York: Random House, Vintage, 1965); and Christopher Lasch, "The Waning of Private Life," *Salmagundi*, no. 36 (1977), pp. 3–15.

functional specialization as he or she matures.[29] While there is an important kernel of truth in this assimilation of Tönnies's theory into the language of personal development, Hawley does not explain the social and psychological mechanisms involved in this process of socialization. It seems, however, that the historical role of the modern graded school, which emerged in American cities about the same time society became bifurcated, has been to perform this task. Since the middle of the nineteenth century, the school has served as a bridge between the familial world of gemeinschaft and the world of gesellschaft.

In colonial towns, the school as a setting for social interaction was not much different from the family or any other institution. Boundaries among the town's various social institutions were highly permeable, and educational tasks were rather casually shifted from one to another of these parallel institutions according to need and availability.[30] By the mid-nineteenth century, when the quality of social relations in the middle-class family became distinct from that in other social institutions, a more complicated program of socialization was needed.[31]

In his history of childhood in Europe, Philippe Ariès observes that the "modern family originated at the same time as the school, or at least as the general habit of educating children at school." He remarks later that this development may reflect a parental perception that their "child was not ready for life."[32] Ariès displays little sympathy for this parental attitude. But parents in Europe and, later, the United States may have been addressing the problem of preparing their children for life in a way that Ariès did not consider. The capacity of the family to socialize the child may not have changed, but the society the children would be entering had. The school was needed to *supplement* the family. Its role was not, as

29. Amos Hawley, *Human Ecology* (New York: Ronald, 1950), p. 208.
30. Cremin, *American Education*, p. 237.
31. On the separation of the middle-class family from society, see Kirk Jeffrey, "Family History: The Middle-Class American Family in the Urban Context, 1830–1870" (Ph.D. diss., Stanford, 1972); Demos, "American Family in Past Time"; Sennett, *Families against the City*. None of these writers consider the school as a possible bridge.
32. Ariès, *Centuries of Childhood*, pp. 370, 412.

some contemporary sociologists suggest, to take over the family's educational functions, but rather to perform new ones that the family could not accomplish.[33] The family taught children about community, while the school introduced them to gesellschaft.

Many nineteenth-century commentators recognized this role for the school, and the educational reforms they proposed were often directed toward this end. Object teaching, an important nineteenth-century pedagogical reform that allowed a degree of spontaneous involvement by children in the classroom, was praised for easing the transition of children into the formal learning and work settings characteristic of urban society. Teachers were advised to be gentle with children in order to smooth the transition from the family to the world of formal institutions. The feminization of the teaching force in elementary schools was motivated in part by a belief, founded upon the stereotype of feminine domesticity, that female teachers would provide a natural bridge between the home and the school. When kindergartens were introduced into the urban public school systems toward the end of the nineteenth century, one of the key issues of debate was how familylike the kindergarten experience ought to be. Initially intended to be an extension of the family, kindergartens were gradually redefined as extensions of the educational bureaucracy. Indeed, the language of family is apparent in nearly all the policy debates surrounding the establishment of the urban public school systems in the nineteenth century.[34]

Here an interesting contrast emerges between Catholic parochial and public education. Catholic schools, which sought an educational style and substance nearer to family ways than was characteristic of the public schools, may have been less effective in

---

33. If this is true, it is essential that the traditional functions of the family not be sacrificed in any modern adaptation of the family. For a devastating critique of contemporary sociological thinking on this point, see Lasch, "Waning of Private Life."

34. See Bender, *Toward an Urban Vision*, pp. 149–151; Daniel Calhoun, *The Intelligence of a People* (Princeton: Princeton University, 1973), pp. 66, 122, 312–314; Michael B. Katz, *The Irony of Early School Reform: Educational Innovation in Mid-Nineteenth Century Massachusetts* (Cambridge: Harvard University, 1968), pp. 56–62; Marvin Lazerson, *Origins of the Urban School: Public Education in Massachusetts, 1870–1915* (Cambridge: Harvard University, 1971), chap. 2.

socializing children for effective participation in America's large-scale social and economic institutions.[35]

To assert the possible role of the school as a bridge between communal and noncommunal networks is, however, only a beginning. We must press our inquiry further and specify what distinguishes the school experience from that in the family. We must also assess what each contributes to socialization. Although historians presently offer little information on this question, recent research in the field of social psychology suggests that in a bifurcated society the family cannot effectively teach children the behavior appropriate to public life.[36] Why? Because the structural characteristics of families, schools, and the institutions of our public life fundamentally differ.

Families are small; they are homogeneous in terms of class, ethnicity, and religion; relationships are long-term; and interaction is largely spontaneous. The primary bond is love, and the expression of affection is expected in all social contacts. Finally, there is little emphasis upon success or failure in specific tasks, and the criteria for success are elastic, with different standards depending upon age, sex, and other personal characteristics. Whether one thinks of our society as a ruthless market society or as a meritocracy that confers rewards on the deserving, these family values are not likely to be effective guides to action in the larger world in which we live.[37]

35. On Catholic education, see Robert D. Cross, "Origins of the Catholic Parochial Schools in America," *American Benedictine Review*, 16 (1965): 194–209; Diane Ravitch, *The Great School Wars: New York City, 1805–1973* (New York: Basic, 1974), chaps. 3–9. On the social results upon which I base this suggestion, see Josef J. Barton, *Peasants and Strangers: Italians, Rumanians, and Slovaks in an American City, 1890–1950* (Cambridge: Harvard University, 1975), pp. 145–146; Gerhard Lenski, *The Religious Factor: A Sociological Study of Religion's Impact on Politics, Economics, and Family Life*, rev. ed. (Garden City, N.Y.: Doubleday, Anchor, 1963), pp. 271–279; Stephan Thernstrom, *The Other Bostonians: Poverty and Progress in the American Metropolis* (Cambridge: Harvard University, 1973); and Thomas Kessner, *The Golden Door: Italian and Jewish Immigrant Mobility in New York City, 1880–1915* (New York: Oxford University Press, 1977).

36. What follows is summarized from Robert Dreeben's imaginative and stimulating book, *On What Is Learned in School* (Reading, Mass.: Addison-Wesley, 1968).

37. The conflict between communal or familial values and meritocratic society is the subject of Michael Young's antiutopian novel, *The Rise of the Meritocracy, 1870–2033* (New York: Penguin, 1961).

The school, by contrast, is larger and more heterogeneous in its population; relationships with teachers are shallow and short-lived (a new teacher every year); and interaction is typically in a formal and judgmental context. Grades, rather than emotional bonds, are used to ensure group cohesion and to influence behavior. In fact, the display of emotion or affection is frowned upon in school, as it is in our public lives. There is a great emphasis upon the performance of specific tasks in school, and the standards of performance are explicitly comparative, that is, all fourth graders should be able to do such and such. In this context, children learn the behavior that is appropriate in the impersonal, mobile, competitive, achievement-oriented and task-oriented world of our economic and political lives.[38]

This description of the school and the socialization experience it offers does not imply that an orientation to gemeinschaft is replaced by one more appropriate to the world of gesellschaft. Rather, it explicitly describes an addition to the psychological repertoire of children. Children (and adults) remain members of families even after they are socialized into the larger patterns of society, and they are still able to "sustain appropriate relationships among kinsmen."[39]

Although the family and the school seem to play central roles in the process of dual socialization, this does not preclude the existence of other social relationships that might facilitate the learning of communal ways or of the ways of gesellschaft.[40] The value of the network approach proposed here is that it allows the social analyst to cast a wide net in his or her search for community and the contexts in which individuals are socialized into the ways of gemeinschaft and gesellschaft.

One point, however, must be kept in mind during this search. Analytically, gemeinschaft and gesellschaft can be completely separated as ideal types, but historians and sociologists must expect to

38. Edgar Friedenberg makes a similar point, without fully developing it, in his *Coming of Age in America* (New York: Random House, Vintage, 1965), p. 239.

39. Dreeben, *On What Is Learned in School*, p. 20.

40. The phrase "dual socialization" is used in another but related context, by Valentine, "Deficit, Difference, and Bicultural Models," p. 142.

find a good deal of interpenetration in actual social experience. There are no completely closed social systems in modern society. External networks impinge upon the family (and all other forms of community), and the ways of community often intrude into larger social networks and institutions.[41]

———◆———

The relation of gemeinschaft and gesellschaft cannot be phrased in simple sequential terms; the former does not simply represent the past and the latter the present. They do bear a historical relationship to each other, but this connection is overlaid with a horizontal one that relates them across social space. As we cast our eyes across the social landscape in the past or in the present, we notice networks of gemeinschaft and gesellschaft linking people and institutions together in a complex pattern of interaction. The advent of this new configuration of society in the nineteenth century represents a fundamental transformation in the experience of community in American history, and we still live with the problems and possibilities produced by this societal revolution.

41. This is predicted by Max Weber, *The Theory of Social and Economic Organization,* trans. Talcott Parsons (New York: Free Press, 1964), p. 137. See Arnold Feldman, "The Interpenetration of Firm and Society," in Georges Balandier, ed. *Social Implications of Technological Change* (Paris: Presses Universitaires de France, 1962), p. 186, and Pleck, "Two Worlds in One."

Chapter Five
Epilog: History and Community Today

Social theory in the nineteenth and twentieth centuries has been concerned with the problem of restating the value of community in an urban society increasingly dominated by large-scale organization. The effort to come to terms with community has, in recent American social thought, tended to blur the distinction between community and other social aggregates. The experience of community, as a result, has been identified with institutionally or territorially defined articulations of the general social system, but this resolution of the problem of community violently, if silently, transforms the meaning of community.

In noting the convergence of the ideas of community and organization, Sheldon Wolin has observed: "The nostalgia for the vanished warmth of the simple community and the obsession with the possibilities of large-scale organization are frequently piled on top of each other." Believing that the small, unique, and particularistic units of life that make for the experience of community have been sentenced to death by historical necessity, the most influential twentieth-century sociologists and social philosophers have tried to recapture community by imputing it to large-scale organizations and to locality-based social activity regardless of the quality of human relationships that characterize these contexts. Instead of accepting the dialectical tension between gemeinschaft and gesellschaft envisioned by Tönnies, modern sociologists, who are ostensibly liberal but in fact subscribe to a deeply conservative ideal that favors comprehensive integrating structures of order and equilibrium, "have tried to engraft elements of community onto the main stem of organization, hoping thereby to lessen the contrast between the two."[1]

This intellectual and political solution trivializes community. It markets the illusion of community while evading the realities of modern social life. Among its disadvantages for our common life is its encouragement of an unspecified feeling of loss and emptiness that in turn makes Americans vulnerable to the manipulation of symbols of community—whether in political rhetoric or in advertising copy. The promotional literature of a recent California development called "The Villages" provides an example. The prospective buyer is asked: "Could you find the answer America is looking for . . . in the first rural town of the seventies?" Having thus evoked the communal myth, the writers of the brochure go on to list the "features" that characterize this "community": transportation by golf cart, vegetable gardens, G. E. kitchens, and an "unobtrusive but efficient 24-hour security patrol." This cynical manipulation of symbols of community is perhaps amusing, but it illustrates the corruption of the notion of community, and this example from popular culture does not differ significantly in this respect from the efforts of academic sociologists to describe American business corporations as a community.[2]

This crisis and confusion in American social thought can be traced in part to a misreading of history. The metaphor of social change and community collapse that pervades sociological and much historical thought is highly deterministic and leaves only two alternatives. Community may be left in the past or it must be drained of its essential qualities so that it is compatible with or even a microcosm of the organizational patterns that seem to dominate modern life. This notion of history and social change obviously dis-

1. Sheldon Wolin, *Politics and Vision: Continuity and Innovation in Western Political Thought* (Boston: Little, Brown, 1960), pp. 366, 376.
2. For a discussion of the work of academic theorists, see ibid., chap. 10.

courages significant social action in behalf of community as an independent and distinctive social experience.[3]

The burden of this book, however, has been to offer an alternative understanding of the historical relationship of community and social change, and revisions of the past, we must remember, always imply new visions of the present and future. The historical interpretation I have presented here results in a metaphor of community that both insists upon its distinctiveness as a form of human relations and offers encouragement to anyone who wants to enhance the reality, as opposed to the illusion, of community in our lives.

What we know of American social history refutes the notion of community collapse. The transformation of community seems better to fit the available evidence. Although the bifurcation of society fundamentally altered the structural location of the experience of community, it did not mark its demise in America. The very notion of bifurcation challenges any assertion that narrows the difference between gemeinschaft and gesellschaft, or that makes community a mere appendage of organizational society. Community, as a social form and as an experience, is distinct from organizational life or gesellschaft. Whereas men and women find their lives in modern society framed by interactions in both of these patterns of social relations, the two social phenomena are separate and cannot be assimilated into one.

These observations on community and social change in American history are intended to clarify the location and meaning of community in our own time. I emphatically do not claim to have discovered that, after all, we really do have community in any satisfactory degree. I offer only a way to think seriously about community in a political manner. My account offers a historical framework within which to discern policy alternatives and institutional innovations and to judge the consequences for community of various political and social acts.

---

3. Alvin Gouldner makes a similar argument in respect to the way theorists of bureaucracy have boxed themselves in. See his "Metaphysical Pathos and the Theory of Bureaucracy," *APSR*, 49 (1955): 496–507.

Any appraisal of the current condition of community in America must, I think, conclude that a market orientation, the great symbol of gesellschaft, dominates too much of our lives and that the experience of community does not comprise enough of them. Perhaps because we have accepted the inevitable social thesis of community collapse, we have acquiesced in a market and competitive model of social relations in areas of our lives in which we can legitimately demand community. The image of the past I have sketched suggests that it is possible to think about enhancing community in our lives without falling into the trap of sentimentality. A sense of the past that appreciates the complexity, contingency, and flux woven into the fabric of history defeats the sort of philosophical determinism underlying conventional theory. The study of the past thus liberates us to act in the present.

Yet important limits remain. The kind of community that is available to us is not the enveloping community seventeenth-century New Englanders knew. That is gone forever, but we need not regret it. To define community in such static terms is to foreclose any possibility of community through time. We need new images of community based upon a historical notion of continual transformation. The bifurcation of society fundamentally altered the dimensions of community in America. This societal development has profoundly complicated our lives, but it has also made them richer. The experience of living in two social and psychological worlds, gemeinschaft and gesellschaft, may produce tensions, but it also offers the prospect of a creative disorderliness in the interstices of these imperfectly integrated social forms.

If we can learn to recognize the various dimensions of community that remain in our lives—and the possibility of enhancing these experiences of community—we might be able to overcome the nostalgia and the illusions bound up with many expressions of community in modern America. We hardly need and probably do not want to be trapped in a three-dimensional web of community. We do need a network of relations that constitute community, but these need not extend to all our neighbors or fellow residents of the metropolis. If we can accept this fact, then we might conquer the nostalgic impulse that seeks community and familiarity in all our social relations. Any attempt to make community everything denies the historical reality in which we live. If we seek community everywhere, we guarantee failure for the quest, and this in turn threatens to make the nostalgic desire all the more intense.

To say that the experience of community must be a limited part of our life is not, however, to counsel passiveness. If we want community, we must believe it is possible, and we must insist upon it. The historical lesson that I derive from this study is that such insistence is plausible. Community can survive, as Tönnes and Durkheim knew, within the world of gesellschaft.

With our confidence about the possibility of community secure, we might gain the added benefit of being able to appreciate the actual virtues, in certain situations, of gesellschaft, of the benevolence of impersonality. A more positive evaluation of public life will moderate the destructive elements of the contemporary search for community and intimacy. This point has been made with compelling force by Richard Sennett in his book, *The Fall of Public Man*, where he writes:

> The lack of a strong impersonal culture in the modern city . . . has aroused a passion for fantasized intimate disclosure between people. Myths of an absence of community, like those of a soulless or vicious crowd, serve the function of goading men to seek out community in terms of a created common self. The more the myth of empty impersonality, in popular forms, becomes the common sense of a society, the more will that populace feel morally justified in destroying the essence of urbanity, which is that men can act together, without compulsion to be the same.[4]

Perhaps this phrasing reverses the causal relations. It may be that we have to become more secure about a relatively small network of community and accept its limits before we can embrace public life. Whatever the causal order, however, we must recognize that a negative image of public life in combination with a quest to make a whole city or even a neighborhood or a bureaucratic organization a

4. Richard Sennett, *The Fall of Public Man* (New York: Knopf, 1977), p. 255.

community only spirals frustrations. A truly humane urban life depends upon a complex balance of gemeinschaft and gesellschaft that is itself grounded upon an appreciation of both of these patterns of social relations.

Our public lives do not provide an experience of community. The mutuality and sentiment characteristic of community cannot and need not be achieved in public. We must be careful to distinguish between these two contexts of social experience, and we must choose the proper psychological repertoire for each.

Politics, for example, belongs to the arena of our public lives. It is not necessary to have intimate knowledge about political figures. What is important is an official's position on policies that affect the whole political body. It is policy and not personality or acquaintance that becomes crucial. We do not live in a Greek polis or even in a colonial New England town, and using the standards of such face-to-face politics today would only obscure what we must know in modern political affairs.[5] Whether a president can make toast is irrelevant, as are the beer drinking feats of a president's brother. A president's economic policies and plans are, however, of absolute interest.

A sense of commonweal, rather than community, provides the essential foundation for a vigorous and effective political life. A commonwealth is based upon shared public ideals, rather than upon acquaintance or affection. Personal knowledge of fellow citizens, real or fancied, is not necessary. What is necessary is full political communication that examines the consequences, general and particular, of proposed and enacted public policies.[6] Such public communication undergirds civic responsibility and enables us to determine whether we share a common interest in certain public policies affecting the whole.

In recent years, urban planners, particularly those on the left, have advocated "community control," making the local neighborhood a key unit of political life. Although I have long accepted this

5. Peter Laslett, "The Face to Face Society," in *Philosophy, Politics and Society,* ed. Peter Laslett (Oxford: Blackwell, 1967), pp. 157–184.

6. This notion is developed in an old but not yet outdated book by John Dewey, *The Public and Its Problems* (New York: Holt, 1927).

political idea, the thesis I have presented here suggests two qualifications I would now make. First, the neighborhood may not be a community. The politics of local areas, including small towns, are more likely to be public than communal, and there is nothing wrong with this. Residents of a locality that is not a community still have important locality-based political concerns, and local political participation may call into being a cluster of political symbols, particularistic and general, that will enhance the politics and civility of urban life.

There are, of course, instances in which localities are also communities, but this is rare today. Where it does occur, it is often the result of the economic and political defeat of groups who have been excluded from full participation in the larger society. Hence there is a great danger in much sentimental writing about community control; it verges close to turning a symbol of defeat into the rallying cry of victory.

My second point deals with the dangers of another kind of entrapment. Although local control is important and worth the effort, power and political problems in modern society are more extensive than a neighborhood or a community. In this circumstance, any effort to concentrate one's efforts on neighborhood or community political activity may mask a denial of access to sources of power affecting local life through general policy.

In all of this, it is important to keep in mind the way in which class intersects with community and power. For the poor and weak in our society, the experience of community seldom has any significant connections with the levers of power. For American elites, however, power and community often overlap. Such was the case with George Templeton Strong in 1870, and it undoubtedly is the case with David Rockefeller a hundred years later. A public politics, at decentralized as well as centralized levels, is likely to advantage those whose community does not run to centers of power, and the whole society should benefit from the extension of access to power.

◆

The breaking apart of the local community in the nineteenth century produced a public culture that Americans have not fully accepted. They have not taken to it, in part, because they have mis-understood the changing character of community. By looking for the experience of community in areas that had become public, they found themselves bereft of community and ignorant of public culture. I hope that the interpretation of historical change offered in this book will reassure Americans about the possibility of community and direct their attention to the various contexts where they can seek to enhance it. Perhaps this will in turn enable them to establish more confident relationships with the public culture of cities. I suspect that an assertion of community in those dimensions of our lives characterized by face-to-face and mutual relations will enhance the quality of our public culture by freeing it from judgment on communal criteria.

Index

151